A SIMPLIFIED APPROACH

TO Milton

Y0-CDG-018

PARADISE LOST

PARADISE REGAINED

L'ALLEGRO

IL PENSEROSO

COMUS

LYCIDAS

AEROPAGITICA

and other writings

By Bernard Grebanier

PROFESSOR OF ENGLISH LITERATURE
BROOKLYN COLLEGE

BARRON'S EDUCATIONAL SERIES, INC.

WOODBURY, NEW YORK

CONTENTS

John Milton

(1608-1674)

MILTON IS OUR greatest poet after Shakespeare. But no two poets have less in common. Understanding Shakespeare is above all a profound experience in broadening one's humanity; understanding Milton is a profound experience in deepening one's aesthetic perceptions and widening one's intellectual horizon. Everybody is a potential audience of Shakespeare; only the intellectually cultivated will love Milton. His learning and erudition are greater than that of any other poet on record. And as a literary artist he has exerted the widest of all influences over later poets. You may read his influence in the work of Dryden, Pope, Cowper, Collins, Gray, Wordsworth, Coleridge, Shelley, Keats, Tennyson and Browning.

He was fortunate in his parents. His father, a scrivener by profession, was well-known as a composer of music. His mother was a woman noted for her deeds of charity. Their home was cultivated, well-to-do, and firmly Puritan. They lived on Bread Street, Cheapside, London, and Milton was born there on December 9, 1608. His father early decided that Milton was to have a literary career, and Milton himself tells us: "From twelve years of age I hardly ever left my studies or went to bed before midnight." After studying at St. Paul's School, Milton entered Christ College, Cambridge in 1625.

At Cambridge he decided that he was to be a great poet, a poet who would write such poetry as posterity "should not willingly let die." To that end he felt he must lead a life of austerity and integrity. For not participating in the riots of his school mates, he was affectionately dubbed "the lady of Christ's."

In 1632 he took his M.A. and went to live at his father's new house in the village of Horton, a few miles from London. His literary output up to this time is not very impressive. He had written some Latin verses and a handful of English poems—none of the latter very good. There are a few good lines in his *Ode on the Morning of Christ's Nativity,* (1629); the poem *On Shakespeare* (1630) is better intended than executed; the sonnet *To the Nightingale* (1631) has a certain charm. But Milton himself in his sonnet *On His Being Arrived to the Age of Twenty-three* (1631) realized full well that he had accomplished very little of which he could be proud.

Milton's father, however, had faith in his son and allowed him to continue his studies at Horton from 1632 to 1638. During these years he made himself master of everything worth knowing in the literature of Rome, Greece, Italy, France, Spain, England; and the Bible, the Talmud, and the writings of the early Christian Fathers were perfectly familiar to him. Toward the close of his stay at Horton, Milton's genius began to produce its first important fruits; *L'Allegro* (1631-32) and *Il Penseroso* (1631-32), *Comus* (1634), and *Lycidas* (1637). These great English poems together with the earlier pieces constitute what is known as Milton's "first period."

Ode on the Morning of Christ's Nativity

This devotional poem was begun, Milton tells us, before the sun rose on Christmas Day, as a birthday present to Jesus, when Milton was twenty-one. Ben Jonson, Beaumont, and Drummond had already written verses on the same subject. In this poem the young scholar fell into the Renaissance habit of using pagan references in a depiction of Christ.

The opening stanzas are written in seven lines rhyming *ababbcc,* the first six being in iambic pentameter, the last line in iambic hexameter. The Hymn itself is written in eight-line stanzas rhyming *aabccbdd;* the first, second, third and fourth being in trimeters, the second and fifth being in pentameters, the sixth in tetrameter, and the last line in hexameter.

This is the month and the day in which the Son of God forsook His place at the Father's side to dwell in mortal clay for our redemption. Has not the Heavenly Muse a song to present as a gift to the infant God? Already the Three Wise Men are hastening with their gifts. Outrun them to lay this song lowly at His Feet.

The Hymn

On the winter day on which the Child is born, Nature hides her guilt with snow. Peace, with her harbinger, the olive-bearing dove, descends to the earth. There is no sound of battle. The bird of calm sits brooding on the wave, and the stars stand fixed in steadfast gaze. The sun still conceals himself because of shame at his inferior light before this greater sun. The shepherds sit chatting, unaware that the mighty Pan has come to live among them; suddenly they hear the exquisite sweetness of the angels' choir. Let the spheres ring out their music too so that for once our mortal ears can hear it: such music would make Time run backwards and kill Vanity and Hell; Truth and Justice would return to men. But Fate says this is not to be, for the Babe is not yet on His cross. Now the oracles are dumb; the Delphic shrine of Apollo has no more to say, and the pagan gods are routed. But hush! let our song end: the sleeping Babe needs quiet, as the bright angels sit in service about Him.

On Shakespeare

The tribute to Shakespeare is in sixteen lines of heroic couplets (iambic pentameter rhyming *aa, bb, cc,* etc.) It was printed among other tributes to Shakespeare in the Second Folio edition of the dramatist's works in 1632. The verses are clearly an elaboration of Ben Jonson's famous line in his poem to Shakespeare printed in the First Folio: "Thou art a monument without a tomb." It must be admitted that that one line is rather better than Milton's sixteen. Like his contemporaries, the young poet looked upon Shakespeare's work as the product of natural genius rather than of art.

Shakespeare needs no stones to do him honor. His name needs no pyramid to celebrate it. He himself has built his own monument in his work, which in its naturalness is a rebuke to the labors of other poets. Indeed, reading his lines, we are turned to marble. Kings could well envy such a tomb.

To the Nightingale

The form is that of an Italian sonnet (eight lines rhyming *abbaabba,* and six *cdcdcd*). The nightingale was to remain Milton's favorite bird, and there are many tributes to it throughout his poetry.

O nightingale, singing at eve in the woods' stillness, you fill the lover's heart with hope, portending success to him. If you indeed have that power, sing now before the bird of hate begins to sing my doom. Every year you have sung too late for my relief; yet I, like you, am devoted to the Muse and to Love.

On His Being Arrived to the Age of Twenty-Three

As is usual with Milton, this sonnet is in the Italian form. Here the concluding section rhymes *cdedce.*

Milton could not pretend to himself that the poems he had been writing had any great quality, even though he had promised himself to write the greatest poem in English. This sonnet is astonishing in its revelation of his capacity for self-criticism, while still maintaining the high ideal he had set for himself. The last lines reveal how powerful the Puritan element already was in his makeup.

Time has swiftly stolen my twenty-third year. My days race on but I have no fruits to show for them. My appearance might deceive some into thinking I am even younger, and maturity is even less ripe within me. Yet whatever my lot is to be—be it less or more, sooner or later—it will be such as Heaven directs. If I have the grace to use it so, everything shall be, as ever, in God's hands.

L'Allegro and Il Penseroso

The titles of these two companion pieces are taken from musicology, and mean respectively "the joyful man" and "the thoughtful man." Considered together they are like a musical composition in two movements, the first gay, the second pensive. They are approximately of the same length and each opens with a ten-line introduction banishing the mood hostile to the spirit of the piece. They are both written in the same meter, which for the bulk of each poem is iambic tetrameter rhyming in couplets. Together they record twenty-four hours in the experience of the poet. The Joyful Man and the Thoughtful Man are the same individual, and the poems exhibit two aspects of his temperament. *L'Allegro* opens at dawn and ends at dark; *Il Penseroso* opens there and closes with the new dawn.

L'ALLEGRO

After banishing the spirit of "loathed melancholy," *L'Allegro* welcomes the Goddess of Mirth, Euphrosyne. With her are also invited Jest, Jollity, Sport, Laughter, and Liberty. The poet, as the lark begins his morning song, commences a tour of the day: the cock strutting before the barnyard door; the sounds of hounds and horn on the hill; the sun rising; the ploughman busy over the soil; the milkmaid, the mower, and the shepherd, at their tasks; the flocks on the sunlit meadows; the flowers and brooks; the village cottages; the hayloft; country dances. Then, as daylight fails: the "nutbrown ale"; folk tales at the fireside; the reading of books of romance and the comedies of Shakespeare and Jonson. The poem concludes with a desire to be lapped "in soft Lydian airs":

> "In notes with many a winding bout
> Of linked sweetness long drawn out
> With wanton heed and giddy cunning,
> The melting voice through mazes running,
> Untwisting all the chains that tie
> The hidden soul of harmony."

IL PENSEROSO

After banishing "deluding joys," *Il Penseroso* welcomes the Goddess Melancholy. With her are also invited Peace, Quiet, Fast, Leisure, Contemplation. The poet, as the nightingale sings

> "In her sweetest, saddest plight
> Smoothing the rugged brow of night . . .
> Sweet bird, that shun'st the noise of folly,
> Most musical, most melancholy!"

begins a tour of the night: the woods; the wandering moon shedding its light through *"Heaven's wide, pathless way,"* and on the lawns; the far-off curfew; at home again

> "Where glowing embers through the room
> Teach light to counterfeit a gloom";

the bellman's song; the watcher in the tower of the mysteries of astronomy. Then, the world of books again: the tragedies of the great Greeks, the *Iliad,* the writings of Chaucer, and Spenser's *Faerie Queene*

> "Of forests, and enchantments drear
> Where more is meant than meets the ear . . ."

As Dawn approaches, the poet escapes the morning light by seeking heavy woods and some quiet brook, or else the cathedral where the organ plays and the full-voiced choir sings so as to dissolve him into ecstasy

> "And bring all Heaven before mine eyes."

Comus

This masque was written, as masques often were, for a particular occasion: an entertainment of the family of the Countess of Derby. Henry Lawes, the distinguished composer, to whom Milton later indited a sonnet, wrote the music to Milton's words. Although Milton was familiar with Jonson's masques, his earnestness of moral purpose differs widely from the tradition of court masques. The story presents an allegory on the ideal of chastity which was so dear to Milton. As in *L'Allegro* and *Il Penseroso* Milton again exhibits an Elizabethan grace and delicacy, but the Puritan side of his nature is also in full bloom. This greatest of all English masques asserts in exquisite poetry the doctrine that the virtuous soul is firmly secure in the midst of all violence and evil. Chastity has always been a fervent personal ideal with the young poet, and here he sings a kind of hymn to it.

The allegorical element is strong. The Lady represents Personal Purity; Comus (from the Greek *komos* = revelry) is Vice at its most alluring; the Monsters of Comus are Simple Brutishness; Thyrsis represents the Divine Care of Goodness; the Elder Brother is Mature Understanding, the product of much study; the Younger Brother is Incomplete Faith.

Scene 1: A wild wood. The Attendant Spirit (who later appears as Thyrsis) informs us that the offspring of the noble peer who owns this territory are coming to greet their father, but their road lies through the tangled paths of this dreary forest. Lest their tender youth be imperiled, Jove has sent the Spirit for their defense. Comus, whom Circe bore to Bacchus, is now in this wood, in whose thick shades he waits for the weary traveler to offer him a shining drink. Whoever tastes of it loses his human appearance, and his face becomes changed to that of a wolf, a bear, a tiger, a hog, or some lower animal, without his ever knowing it, and the victim thinks himself more comely than before. Forgetting home, he rolls with pleasure in a sensual sty.

As the Attendant Spirit changes to the guise of a shepherd, he hears the tread of hateful steps, and disappears. Comus enters with his crew, headed like various monsters but with the bodies of men and women. He bears a rod in one hand, a glass in the other. His followers, torches in hand, enter in an unruly noise. It is evening.

Comus bids his crew dance. (The dances were fundamental to the idea of the court masque.) In the midst of the dancing, Comus halts them. He hears chaste steps coming this way. He commands the others to take cover, and begins to weave spells in the air.

The Lady enters. She has heard the sound of merry-making, and, not knowing her way, has come for some direction. Her brothers, when she was too wearied to travel more, went to fetch her some fruit. But they did not return, and she cannot guess where they are. The sounds of revelry towards which she has bent her steps have ceased, and she does not know whether she can make her brothers hear her, but she will try. She sings an exquisite song:

> Sweet Echo, sweetest nymph, that liv'st unseen
>   Within thy airy shell,
>   By slow Meander's margent green. . . .
> Canst thou not tell me of a gentle pair
>   That likest thy Narcissus are? . . .

Comus is enraptured with the song and with the voice that sang it. He speaks to her. Is she, he asks, the goddess of these woods?

Thinking him a shepherd, the Lady reproves him for his flattery, and explains that she was hoping her brothers would hear her. Comus pretends that he has seen two such as he she describes, plucking some grapes. They were so beautiful, he was sure they could not have been mortal. Comus offers to lead her to them in the morning. In the meantime he can show her to a safe lowly lodging for the night. She gratefully accepts.

Scene 2: The two brothers, who have lost their path, enter. The stars are dim and the moon is clouded over. The Younger Brother is worried about their lost sister. She may be chilled by the night, frightened, or within the grip of hunger. The Elder Brother chides him for imagining evils that may not exist. Besides, their sister is a creature of virtue; and virtue can see by its own light even without sun or moon:

> Virtue could see to do what virtue would
> By her own radiant light, though sun and moon
> Were in the flat sea sunk. . . .
> He that has a light within his own clear breast
> May sit i' the center,* and enjoy bright day
> But he that hides a dark soul and foul thoughts,
> Benighted walks under the midday sun;
> Himself is his own dungeon.

(This is an expression of what was central to Milton's religious beliefs, and is a conviction basic to the ethical meaning of *Paradise Lost.*) Their sister is not so defenseless as the Younger Brother thinks: she has her chastity to protect her. The Elder Brother delivers a discourse on the safeguards provided by Heaven to the pure of soul. Charmed, the Younger Brother exclaims: "How charming is divine philosophy!"

They hear a far-off halloo, and the Elder Brother answers it. It is the Attendant Spirit, now habited as the shepherd Thyrsis, and he joins them. Thyrsis asks after the Lady, and they tell him she is lost. Thyrsis now tells them about Comus, who lives within these woods, and of the mischief he works upon the traveler.

This evening, after his flocks were in the fold, Thyrsis heard the rout of Comus' followers; then he heard later in the midst of the night's silence a lovely voice:

> I was all ear,
> And took in such strains that might create a soul
> Under the ribs of death.

* i.e., the center of the universe.

He recognized it as the voice of their sister. He ran to meet her, but soon saw that Comus had already encountered her; he overheard her telling Comus how she had lost her brothers. In fear of Comus, Thyrsis had run off.

The Younger Brother demands to know where his brother now can find confidence. The Elder Brother will not retract a syllable of what he says. (Here Milton delivers a wonderful expression of faith in the inevitable triumph of Good over Evil:)

> This I hold firm:
> Virtue may be assailed, but never hurt,
> Surprised by unjust force, but not enthralled;
> Yea, even that which mischief meant most harm,
> Shall in the happy trial prove most glory:
> But evil on itself shall back recoil,
> And mix no more with goodness; when at last,
> Gathered like scum, and settled to itself,
> It shall be in eternal restless change,
> Self-fed, and self consumed: if this fail,
> The pillared firmament is rottenness,
> And earth's base built on stubble.

The Elder Brother will find Comus and force him to give their sister back. But Thyrsis assures him his sword will do little good. Against Comus' enchantments only the herb called "haemony" will make one safe. Of this Thyrsis will pluck them some. What they must do is break Comus' glass, pour the liquor on the ground, and seize his wand.

Scene 3: A stately palace, soft music, tables spread with dainties. Comus places the Lady in an enchanted chair, offers her his glass, which she rejects, and prevents her rising. He warns her that a wave of his wand will render her immobile. She replies that nothing he does can touch the freedom of her mind. He asks her why she is vexed with him; why does she refuse the drink that will refresh her? She answers that she knows he is lying again. Is this the lowly cottage he promised? And who are these hideous monsters? She would accept nothing at his hands, even if the drink were one for Juno:

> None
> But such as are good men can give good things.

Comus now advances a sophistical argument. Why is Nature so profuse in her bounties if not to satisfy the curious taste? If all the world insisted upon being temperate, the All-giver would be unthanked, not half his riches known. Let her not be deceived by the word "virginity." Beauty must not be hoarded; the Good consists in mutual bliss. If she lets time slip by she will wither like an unplucked rose.

The Lady responds that she would disdain to answer him but that he might imagine that he has enchanted her judgment. If every man had enough, there would be no excess in Nature. Those who are gluttons have no thought for Heaven. But what is the use of her continuing? Comus has no way of understanding the sublimity and high mystery of chastity. Let him enjoy his own wit; he is not fit to hear himself convinced.

Comus, despite himself, is somewhat moved by her eloquence. But he tries again, this time attempting to force her to drink. The Brothers rush in with their swords drawn, seize his glass, and dash it to the ground. The Monsters try to resist, but they are driven off with Comus.

Thyrsis enters. He regrets that they forgot to seize his wand too. With it they could free the Lady from his spells, who sits there like stone. But he remembers another expedient. Sabrina, a gentle nymph, the goddess of the river (Severn), is always beneficent. She is devoted to maidenhood, and will be swift to unlock Comus' spells. Thyrsis summons her in a beautiful song:

> Sabrina fair,
>   Listen where thou art sitting
> Under the glassy, cool, translucent wave. . . .

Sabrina rises with her water nymphs, and answers in another song. At Thyrsis' request, she frees the Lady from her seat.

The masque ends in happy dance and song, with a charming compliment to the Earl of Bridgewater, in whose honor the piece was presented on September 29, 1634. The final lines express again the leading idea of the poem: the virtuous mind is safe from the attacks of evil—

> "Love virtue, she alone is free;
> She can teach ye how to climb
> Higher than the sphery chime;
> Or if Virtue feeble were,
> Heaven itself would stoop to her."

Lycidas

Called by many critics the greatest achievement of English lyrical poetry, this elegy was written upon the death of a fellow-alumnus of Milton's, Edward King, who was drowned in the Irish Sea in 1637. A group of King's former school mates at Cambridge issued a commemorative volume titled *Obsequies to the Memory of Mr. Edward King* (1638). It was in this limited publication that *Lycidas* first appeared. Heretofore, of his great poems only *Comus* had been published, and that anonymously.

Lycidas is not an expression of personal grief (personal grief was to be eloquent in Milton's next important poem, the Latin *Epitaphium Damonis*), but rather a record of the thoughts that King's death evoked in the poet. King had written verses himself and had prepared himself for the Church. These two facts of the dead man's career form the basis for what Milton had to say. Outwardly the poem is written in the tradition of pastoral poetry, and more particularly in the tradition of the pastoral elegy as exhibited in the ancient Greek *Lament for Bion* by Moschus. The poet is spoken of as a shepherd. But Milton introduces the innovation of identifying the Christian idea of shepherd (pastor) as meaning *priest*. In a wonderful fusion of pagan and Christian tradition, Milton makes his elegy the occasion for a scathing attack on the corruptions of the clergy in his time, with parenthetical thrusts of scorn at his trivial contemporaries, the Cavalier poets.

Samuel Johnson, who disliked all pastoral poetry, made the one outstandingly foolish judgment of his career, in dismissing *Lycidas* as a work of art. He said its "diction is harsh, the rhymes uncertain, and the numbers unpleasing,"—a testimony to the fact that Johnson was deaf to the refinements of English poetry at its subtlest, for *Lycidas* is an exquisite piece of music from the first line through the last. Moreover, Johnson was upset at the mingling of "trifling fictions" with "the most awful and sacred truths, such as ought never to be polluted with such irreverent combinations." That pronouncement can only mean that Johnson failed to grasp the noble idea at the center of the poem: Milton's definition of the high function of a poet.

Milton had shared with King a love of nature and of poetry, and a hope for fame. The death of his college friend causes him to ask himself in *Lycidas* some questions highly important to a man who was resolved to write the greatest poem in English: If Death can come so suddenly, of what use are such high idealism and purposes? Would it not be better to live for the joy of the senses (as the Cavalier poets even then were doing)? Milton confronts these doubts honestly and emerges with an answer.

Lycidas opens with the poet's declaration that he has been forced to write poetry (the "laurel" is the symbol of poetry; the "myrtle" and "ivy" are symbols of death) before he was ready to do so again, because of the death of his friend Lycidas (i.e., King). He must sing for Lycidas, for he was a poet too. Milton invokes the Muses, and thinks wistfully that perhaps some day a fellow poet will sing for him when he in turn is dead.

He and Lycidas were nursed upon the same hill (i.e., they went to Cambridge together); their tasks were the same, they made poems together, and old Damoetas (probably some college tutor) encouraged their efforts.

But all the world is changed now that you are gone, Lycidas, and all Nature mourns for you. Why did not the nymphs, who used to love to hear Lycidas' song, save him. Where were they when he was drowned? Ah, that is a vain question! How could they have saved him, when the Muse Calliope herself could not save her enchanting son Orpheus from being torn to pieces at the hands of the Thracian women?

Alas! What is the use of giving one's best to the profession of poetry (the "shepherd's trade"), and devoting oneself exclusively to it? Would it not be better to enjoy oneself in amorous exploits (i.e., as do the Cavalier Poets)? It is fame which encourages the poet to scorn pleasure and work hard at his art. But just as he seems about to reap the reward of fame, Death comes along to end his life.—"But not his praise," the God of Poetry (Phoebus) whispers into Milton's trembling ears. "Fame is not a plant that grows on mortal soil. It lives by the will of God. As He pronounces on every deed, so expect your fame in heaven."

And now Triton asks the waves and winds how this mishap to Lycidas occurred. They cannot answer, nor can Aelous himself, god of the winds. The sea was calm that day. It was the cursed ship which was responsible for the death of Lycidas. Next Camus (a personification of the river Cam at Cambridge) comes to lament Lycidas.

The last of the mourners is Saint Peter (the founder of the Christian Church—he is here because young King was a clergyman), who speaks sternly: How well I could have spared instead of you those who become clergymen for their bellies' sake! They are blind mouths, who know nothing about the duties of a shepherd. [Here Milton deliberately identifies the classic tradition that shepherd = poet, with the Christian tradition that shepherd = priest. In other words, the poet—like the Old Testament prophets—should be a priest too. This is the great point which Johnson, in his indignation, missed. It is one of the boldest strokes in English poetry, and gives us a clear idea of Milton's conception of his own obligations to the world.] They do not care what happens to their flocks, for they are doing well for themselves. And when they want to, they contrive to sing their empty heartless songs. [Milton is again referring to his contemporaries, the Cavalier poets, some of whom were, indeed, of the clergy.] The hungry flock looks up to them and receives no nourishment, while every day the Roman Church wins new converts. But the instrument of revenge [the "two-handed engine" = the two houses of Parliament?] is ready to smite and dispense with them.

To atone for the severity of the St. Peter passage, the poet now outdoes himself in an exquisite passage which enumerates all the flowers of the field which will strew the poetic hearse of Lycidas.

Where can the bones of Lycidas lie now? Beyond the Hebrides? Or near Land's End in Cornwall? Where have they been washed by the deep?

The lament for King concludes with a burst of glorious poetry:

> "Weep no more, woeful shepherds, weep no more,
> For Lycidas, your sorrow, is not dead,
> Sunk though he be beneath the watery floor;
> So sinks the day-star in the ocean bed,
> And yet anon repairs his drooping head,
> And tricks his beams, and with new-spangled ore
> Flames in the forehead of the morning sky."

So Lycidas has arisen anew, and in Heaven mixes with the blessed, who sing and move in their glory, and wipe the tears forever from his eyes.

The poem ends with a touching epilogue. The poet has been singing all day. At the end of his song the sun is setting. He rises, and plucks his cloak about him. Tomorrow he will be singing of other things. (This is a hint of the "great poem" to which Milton thought he might now be able to turn.)

In April, 1638, Milton left Horton for a tour of the continent.

He visited Paris, Nice, Genoa, Leghorn and Pisa. At Florence, the great center of cultural activity in Italy, he made many friendships among prominent Italian writers. He went on to Siena, Rome and Naples. He was about to proceed to the East when he learned of civil discords brewing in England, and felt it was his duty to come home. When he arrived in England he discovered that his best friend, Charles Diodati, had died. In memory of their friendship Milton wrote his greatest Latin poem, the *Epitaphium Damonis,* which may be considered the last poem in his first period. The first period of Milton's career may be summarized as exhibiting him as a son of the Elizabethans, interested primarily in love of beauty and learning, with the Puritan side of his nature present but not emphatic.

Milton's Second Period

The "second period" of Milton's career (1641-1654) finds him so much the Puritan that he writes very little poetry. On his return from the continent he settled in London and began to tutor. In 1641 begins a long period of pamphleteering in the service of democracy and Puritanism. He had already decided that he must write a great poem. But he felt that his duty to his country required his laying aside his own creative ambitions and placing his talents in the service of those who were fighting for liberty. His first piece of argumentative prose was *Of Reformation* (1641), an attack on the political corruption of the clergy in the English Church, and a plea for democracy in the structure of the Church. In the same year he wrote *Of Prelatical Episcopacy,* an argument to prove the superiority of the Presbyterian system of Church government; and *Animadversions,* an attack on Bishop Hall (the Character writer), a powerful prelate of the English Church. *The Reason of Church Government* (1642) is Milton's longest ecclesiastical tract, and urges the separation of Church and State. The last of the anti-Episcopal pamphlets, published the same year, was *An Apology,* an answer to personal attacks on him made by the opposition.

In 1643, Milton went into the country on a commission for his father, met Mary Powell, daughter of a Cavalier family, and married her. After a month with her he left her presumably to make her farewells to her friends. Once he was in London, however, she refused to rejoin him. The sudden failure of his marriage turned Milton's thoughts to the subject of divorce. In 1643, 1644 and 1645 he issued four tracts on divorce: *The Doctrine and Discipline of Divorce, The Judgment of Martin Bucer, Tetrachordon,* and *Colasterion.* It is Milton's view in these pamphlets that all that should be necessary to disrupt a marriage tie is the willingness of both parties to separate. He believed incompatibility to be a better argument for divorce than adultery. Naturally, Milton was bitterly attacked for these revolutionary opinions. It is interesting that in spite of his stand, when his wife pleaded with him to be taken back in 1645, he was willing to have her return. She bore him three daughters and died in 1652.

Milton's defense of divorce began a series that continued his defense of personal liberty, as he had already defended religious liberty. His next important tract was *Of Education* (1644), in which he urges the supplementing of books with personal contact and practical experience.

Areopagitica

The same year saw the publication of his most important treatise, *Areopagitica,* a noble defense of the freedom of the press. Parliament had passed a law requiring all books to be licensed by a censor. The Presbyterians, now in control, were attempting to bring all of England to their way of thinking. Milton was indignant that a Puritan party should revive Charles I's licensing act. The *Areopagitica* was addressed to Parliament in the hope of convincing it to repeal the act. It is a magnificent example of the classic oration. (The title is derived from a speech addressed by Isocrates to the Athenian court of the Areopagus.) Milton argues that only enemies of truth have ever tried to crush a free press, and that it is impossible to make men good by external restraints. Most of all he is concerned by the danger to the pursuit of truth. He has complete faith in the ability of people who can read to find their own salvation. The *Areopagitica* has remained a source of inspiration to all who have fought for freedom of speech and of the press, and Milton's arguments were to be repeated in France in the era preceding the French Revolution.

Milton's arguments are, on the whole, unanswerable:

1] Who is to choose the censors? What man is wise or good enough to censor the reading of others?

2] To the pure all things are pure; to the evil all things become corrupt. The good will not be corrupted; nothing can prevent the evil from being corrupted—if it will not be a book, it will be something else.

3] In a world where good and evil exist side by side, it is necessary to be able to recognize evil so as to avoid it.

4] The best ideas when they first appear are likely to be un-
palatable at first. Who can tell from what quarter the best ideas
may emanate? There must be no possible choking, therefore, of
any avenues of expression.

5] In a free society nothing is less desirable than a starched
conformity of opinion. Censorship can only operate to stifle the
free interchange of ideas, so necessary to the health of liberty.

The struggle between the King and Parliament now came to
a head. Charles was tried, and, in February 1649, beheaded. Milton's next tract begins his series on political liberty. In *Of the
Tenure of Kings and Magistrates* (1649) he attempted to quiet
the public's reaction of fear to the beheading of Charles. His argument was that a people may end whenever they see fit the rule
of their monarch. The new Commonwealth recognized the im-
portance of Milton's service in this pamphlet, and appointed him
Latin Secretary in March 1649. Among his many duties was to
defend his country against the many attacks which the monarchies
of Europe were aiming at it in print. His energies were now
completely absorbed in this work. *Eikonoklastes* (1649) was an
answer to a monarchist attempt to paint Charles as a martyred
saint. This kind of work and the mass of State correspondence
which it was his duty to answer resulted in Milton's losing the
sight of one eye in 1650. A very dangerous book against the
Commonwealth now appeared, but Milton was threatened with
the loss of the sight of his other eye if he did not cease his labors.
Fully aware of the risk he was taking, he answered in *The Defense
of the English People* (1651). In 1652 he was a blind man.

Blindness, terrible to all its victims, must have been tragic
beyond description to a poet who loved books more than anyone
we know of, and who was, moreover, an expert musician on the
organ. Yet, nowhere in Milton do we read of regret for having
sacrificed his eyesight. When another enemy of the Republic,
learning of Milton's blindness, attacked him in particular, and
cited Milton's affliction as God's punishment for his part in the
execution of Charles, Milton dictated his spirited *Second Defense
of the English People* (1654), which contains a noble defense of
his conduct. The *Second Defense of the English People* is in one
respect Milton's most interesting prose work, for it contains a
long and very informative autobiographical section.

Milton continued his defense of the Republic despite his blindness. His later treatises are: *Pro Se Defensio,* (1655), *A Treatise*

of Civil Power (1659), *Considerations* (1659)—and, in 1660, when Charles Stuart was preparing to return to assume his father's throne, Milton's warning against the restoration of the Stuarts, *The Ready and Easy Way to Establish a Free Commonwealth.* His prose works also include a *History of Britain* (1646-1660), *Of Christian Doctrine* (1655-1660), *Of True Religion* (1672), a Latin grammar, a Latin dictionary, and a book on Russian.

In the meantime, because of his blindness, he had retired from active service in the Council. He married Katherine Woodcock in November of 1656, but she died in February 1658 with the daughter to which she had given birth. It was on her that he wrote his most touching sonnet.

It is ironical that it was his blindness which gave him the freedom again to take up his vocation of poet. His third, and last period, may be said to begin in 1655 with his great sonnets, and includes his major works: *Paradise Lost, Paradise Regained,* and *Samson Agonistes.* But these great works were not written in peace. At the Restoration Milton was forced to remain in hiding for some time because of his services to the Commonwealth. He was even arrested for a while, but was released on the payment of a heavy fine. His declining years were embittered by the neglect and dislike of his three daughters. Needing someone to take care of him, in 1663 he married Elizabeth Minshull, who was thirty years his junior. His will left his estate to her because of the unkindness of his daughters.

Milton had written a number of sonnets before this, including one to Henry Lawes, the musician, and one to Cromwell. But the most important of his sonnets are three written in 1655, when he had been blind for three years: *On His Blindness, To Cyriack Skinner,* and *On the Late Massacre in Piedmont;* and the sonnet written in 1658, *On His Deceased Wife.* As usual with him, they are written in the Italian form.

On His Blindness

Milton asks the question: "Does God expect me to continue my labors in God's cause even though I am blind?"

When I consider how I am blind before half my days are over and that, like the well-meaning but foolish servant who buried his talent in the ground (See *Matthew* 25:14-30), I put my talent to no use, though I am anxious to serve God—I ask, "Does God expect me to work without my eyes?" But Patience reminds me that God has no need of mortal help. Those who bear his mild yoke, serve him best. *"They also serve who only stand and wait."*

To Cyriack Skinner

This poem was addressed to a close friend.

It is three years today since these eyes of mine, though they seem to others normal enough, have lost their sight. But I do not argue against the will of Heaven, but bear up. What supports me? The knowledge that I lost my sight in the defense of liberty—a knowledge that could lead me through the world without a better guide.

(Milton wrote another, less important, sonnet *To Cyriack Skinner,* encouraging him to relax occasionally from his serious endeavors.)

On the Late Massacre in Piedmont

Containing the most resounding music of any of Milton's sonnets, this is his first experiment in the "organ tone" which was to lift *Paradise Lost* to a unique place in world poetry.

In April, 1655, the Duke of Savoy, in an excess of religious enthusiasm, massacred the Protestants living in the mountains of Piedmont. As England's great Protestant poet, Milton here nobly exclaims:

> Avenge O Lord, thy slaughtered saints, whose bones
> Lie scattered on the Alpine mountains cold . . .

He ends with the wish that their martyred blood may fertilize the Italian soil that from these may grow a hundredfold of others to oppose the Pope.

On His Deceased Wife

Milton was already blind when in 1656 he married Katherine Woodcock. He had loved her, but had never seen her. When she died in 1658 he wrote this poignant sonnet.

I thought I saw my late saintly wife, brought to me all in white, and looking as I trust to have full sight of her in Heaven. Her face was veiled, but to my imagined sight I read love, sweetness, and goodness there.

> But, oh! as to embrace me she inclined,
> I waked, she fled, and day brought back my night.

Paradise Lost

Here is the great poem which Milton for many years knew he was to write. During the years of political activity, he had been seeking about for a subject, and for a time toyed with the idea of writing on the Arthurian legend. But eventually he chose a far greater subject—the Fall of Adam and Eve from God's grace, and through them, the fall of the human race. The poem is, of course, entirely the work of a blind man. It was composed as Milton lay abed nights, and dictated during the day to his secretary.

When it was issued to the public, in 1665, its sale was small; nevertheless, it has exerted a greater influence on the history of English poetry than any other poem ever written. It was Milton's own testament of faith in the Puritan philosophy, and sent into the world in days when the public was mocking everything Milton had fought for.

No other poem contains such treasures of learning. To the outlines of the story the Bible, the Talmud, the Church Fathers contributed. The structure and tragic tone of the poem are indebted to Homer and Virgil. But everywhere one will find transfigured for Milton's own purposes a world of literary tradition: Greek mythology, the Scriptures, Ovid, Ariosto, Tasso, Spenser, and many Renaissance writers in Italian, Latin, French and English. The reference in Milton to the lore of learning is not decoration, it is the very tissue of his thinking. The endless richness of allusion deepens his ideas at every turn.

No story of such vastness was ever told by a poet before as in this epic. The immensities of the physical universe are the background for the events. We are now in Hell, now in Heaven, now in the vast depths of Chaos, now in the ten concentric spheres which, (in the Ptolemaic System of Astronomy), encircle the Earth, now in the Garden of Eden.

Milton planned his masterwork over a period of more than a quarter of a century. When he was only nineteen, and at college, the young poet declared (in *A Vacation Exercise*) that he would write an English poem

> Such where the deep transported mind may soar
> Above the wheeling poles, and at Heav'ns door
> Look in.

His subject would have the dignity, he said, of Homer's epics. In his *Elegy VI,* written in Latin during December, 1629, he decided that to write such a poem he must live a pure life. The first lines of *Lycidas* (1638) imply an unwillingness to be writing while his great poem was not yet begun; the lines put in St. Peter's mouth indicate his idea of the high function of a poet; the last line promises, once more, the great poem to come.

Thus far Milton was thinking of using the Arthurian legends as his subject. Next year, in the *Epitaphium Damonis,* he hinted that he had already begun to work on those stories.

But in *The Reason of Church Government* (1642) he declared that he could not decide upon the form of his great poem. Should it be an epic like Homer's, a short epic like *The Book of Job,* or a tragedy in the manner of Sophocles? (In the end, he wrote a masterpiece in each of these forms: *Paradise Lost, Paradise Regained,* and *Samson Agonistes,* respectively.) Also, should he choose a subject from British lore or from the Bible?

Soon after his return from Italy he began to set down a list of almost one hundred subjects from those two sources, on any one of which he might write the great work. Gradually he seems to have decided upon the Fall of Man as his subject, though at first he planned to write it as a drama.

From 1641 he had been engaged in the controversies of his country on great and immediate issues. Though he no doubt was constantly thinking of the poem he felt called upon to write, he had no leisure to work on it. It was only blindness that eventually gave him that.

Almost a lifetime of integrity and self-discipline went into the composition of *Paradise Lost.* Much of it was composed after Charles II had been restored to the throne. Although everything for which he had given his talents and sacrificed his eyes was now being derided and mocked at, he had no qualms about the cause for which he had sacrificed so much, and continued on his magnificent poem undismayed. It was completed by 1665, and published in 1667. Milton received for it the great sum of ten pounds!

Though Milton's was the chief voice of Puritanism, he was no narrow Calvinist. Indeed, he rejected the characteristic Puritan notion of mankind's being an aggregation of sinners in the hands of an angry God. At the root of his poem is an anti-Calvinist philosophy. The Calvinists believe that man was predestined from birth to salvation or damnation and that nothing the individual might do could alter that predestinated fate. But Milton particularly stresses throughout *Paradise Lost* the belief that man is free to choose between right and wrong. His Adam was created free to eat or not to eat the forbidden fruit.

In all other respects the poem is staunchly Puritan in its ideas. Throughout there is an insistence that God is to be found in the heart, not in churches, and that Knowledge is an essential for the life of virtue.

As complex as is Milton's art, so simple is his story. One does not lose the thread of it or its thought for a moment. However, although his medium is blank verse, as was that of Shakespeare, nothing could be further from Shakespeare's language than Milton's. Shakespeare employed the colloquial and idiomatic diction and rhythms of English discourse. For Milton's purposes something entirely different was necessary. His preference for the unusual and learned in diction and for the use of words in their original sense is part of Milton's sublimity. For, close to the Latin as he often is, his style is all his own, and it became a model for English poetry thereafter, beginning at once with his contemporary, Dryden, and continuing through Pope, Thomson, Cowper, Wordsworth, Coleridge, Shelley, Keats, and Tennyson. Professor Havens has singled out the following characteristics of Milton's manner:

1] The inversion of the normal order of words and phrases:
                    Him the Almighty Power
            Hurled headlong flaming.

                                    (I, 44)
2] The omission of words superfluous to the meaning:
            Fallen cherub, to be weak is miserable,
            Doing or suffering.

                                    (I, 157)
3] Parenthesis and apposition:
            Of Abbana and Pharphar, lucid streams.
                                    (I, 469)
            But what if he our Conqueror (whom I now

Of force believe Almighty, since no less
Than such could have o'erpowered such force as ours)
Have left us this our spirit and strength entire . . .

(I, 143)

4] The use of one part of speech for another: *dark with excessive bright; the great consult began; since created man.*

5] Latinisms and archaisms:

Reassembling our afflicted (in Latin = "cast down") *Powers.*

(I, 186)

No wonder, fall'n such a pernicious (in Latin = death-dealing) *highth.*

(I, 282)

Ammiral (= admiral ship. The spelling was than archaic.)
Frequent (in Latin = crowded).
Fact of Arms (= deed of arms).

6] Fondness for exotic proper names:

Down to the golden Chersonese, or where
The Persian in Ecbatan sat, or since
In Hispahan, or where the Russian Ksar
In Mosco, or the Sultan in Bizance,
Turchestan-born.

(XI, 392)

7] Unusual compound epithets, like those in Homer: *heavenly-born; night-warbling bird.*

Each of these devices can, of course, be found in poets preceding Milton, but in no other poet, before or since, are they all found so frequently.

For the background of his poem, Milton needed no less than the whole of the created universe. Though he was quite familiar with the new heliocentric conception, it was too unmanageable as a setting, and he therefore chose the older, geocentric idea of the universe.

The following is the scheme of Milton's cosmology:

1] Before the revolt of Lucifer, Space was divided into two parts: above was Heaven, the Empyrean, the home of God and the angels; below was uncreated Chaos.

2] Because of the revolt of Lucifer and his cohorts, God created at the bottom of Chaos a region known as Hell, to receive the falling angels.

3] Then to establish a place for the home of man, God created the universe, which Milton throughout calls "the World." (What we call the world is named either "the Earth" or "the

Center" in the poem.) This created universe or World has fixed at its center the Earth. (Hell is three times the distance from the Earth that the Earth is from the Empyrean.) Around the fixed Earth revolve the ten concentric spheres, in this ascending order: the spheres of the Moon, of Mercury, of Venus, of the Sun, of Mars, of Jupiter, of Saturn, of the Fixed Stars, then the Crystalline Sphere, and finally the Primum Mobile ("First Mover"), which imparts motion to the other nine spheres. The Primum Mobile is encased in a hard shell, sheltering the World from Chaos, which surrounds it. This World hangs by a golden ladder from the Empyrean.

Before discussing the sources of *Paradise Lost,* we cannot sufficiently stress the fact that this incomparable poem was the work of a blind man. No other literary composition approaches it in the richness of literary reference, but none of it is the product of Milton's searching through books to adorn his poem—that would manifestly have been impossible to a blind man. If there is an endless literary wealth of reference in the poem, it is because it was, to begin with, inside Milton. It was the very mode of his thinking. Probably no one in history had read as much as he. Certainly no one else has so converted learning into beauty.

The basic plot of *Paradise Lost* comes from the few lines in *Genesis* 2. But Milton has used as his authority countless passages in the Bible for his accounts of the birth of Adam, the birth of Eve, the creation of the universe. As a matter of fact, the concluding books of the poem in which Michael delivers his prophecies to Adam, is a brilliant summary of a vast amount of the Old and New Testaments. The fall of Satan has as its Biblical authority *Revelation* 12. But Milton also put to good use the Apocryphal *Book of Enoch,* and the *Book of Tobit,* for details concerning Satan and Raphael, respectively. He was thoroughly familiar with the rabbinical commentaries in The Talmud, which had elaborated on Adam, Eve, and Lucifer. Milton was also deeply read in the writings of the Church Fathers, Latin and Greek. He knew many other Jewish writings such as those of Josephus and Maimonides. Saint Augustine's *City of God* was in his thoughts when writing about the Fall itself. This is only a partial list of the religious backgrounds of *Paradise Lost.*

For the form of his poem, he looked naturally to Homer and Virgil. As an art-epic, *Paradise Lost* follows the epic conventions, which were based upon Virgil's deliberate imitation of Homer.

These epic conventions include:

1] The statement of the subject in the opening lines.
2] The appeal to the Muse for inspiration, at the beginning, and at important moments when there is a shift in the action.
3] Beginning the story in the middle of the action (in Horace's phrase: to begin *in medias res*).
4] The enumeration of the host of warriors.
5] The war-council of the leaders.
6] The alternation of scenes on earth with scenes in Heaven.
7] The use of long dramatic dialogue.
8] The use of extended descriptive passages.
9] The elaborate simile ("the epic simile").
10] The allegorical episode.
11] Epic games.
12] The description of technical enterprises.
13] The messenger from Heaven sent to warn a mortal.
14] The business and conduct of war.
15] Prophecy.
16] Significant dreams.

There were, naturally, many literary treatments of the Fall of Man antecedent to Milton, some of them going back to the Dark Ages. Among the works which Milton may have known are two Renaissance dramas, Andreini's *Adamo* (published 1613), written in Italian, and Grotius' *Adamus Exul* (1601), written in Latin. But the indebtedness, if any, is general rather than specific.

To trace all the influence upon this poem would be impossible, considering the scope of Milton's reading. What is most fascinating about him is that he is probably not only the most learned but also the most original poet England ever had.

It is no doubt unfortunate that many modern readers never get beyond the opening two books of *Paradise Lost,* which are normally found in college anthologies. It is likely that the absurd notion that despite himself Milton had made his villain, Satan, the hero, could not otherwise be held, as it is so widely. It suited the prejudices of the Romantic Poets to distort the poem by saying this —to see Satan as a kind of prototype of Byron, as Byron did himself; but any modern person saying this is only thereby declaring either that he never got beyond Book II, or else has read the other portions superficially.

In the early books of *Paradise Lost* Satan emerges as the most heroic figure, proud tragic, unwilling to submit to defeat. But that is because Milton was too great an artist not to do full justice to his villain. The hero of his tragedy is Adam, who at first may seem less magnificent than Satan. But as Satan's character becomes more and more debased through his evil plans and actions, Adam's, somewhat because of his human frailty, rises higher in comparison. At the end, because Adam faces his guilt, he emerges in truly heroic proportions. The relations between Adam and Eve, especially before the Fall, are described with charm and with many touching details. Indeed, *Paradise Lost* contains an almost endless variety of poetry: the tragic, the luxuriantly descriptive, the tender, the intellectual, the exalted.

It has sometimes been said that the only parts of this poem which are a failure are those which take place in Heaven. The observation is certainly untrue for the many seraphic outbursts in song of the Angels. But it must be admitted that by definition it is impossible to represent Deity with any human qualities, and it is not surprising, therefore, that the passages in which God speaks are too severe and cold in comparison with the rest of the poem. But those passages, after all, are few in number. *Paradise Lost* is the greatest single accomplishment in English non-dramatic poetry.

The blank verse of *Paradise Lost* has such sweep, grandeur and power as have won for it the description of "Milton's organ tone."

BOOK ONE

Sing, Heavenly Muse, of Man's first disobedience and of the forbidden fruit which brought woe and death into the world until Christ restore us. I ask your aid for my song which I intend shall outsoar the pagan epics, for it deals with matters never yet attempted. Inspire me that

> I may assert eternal Providence,
> And justify the ways of God to men.

What caused our first parents, who except for one prohibition were lords of the world, to transgress God's will? It was Satan, who deceived the mother of mankind; he was then cast out of Heaven for his rebellion, with all his rebel angels.

(We now begin our story in the middle of the events, with this magnificent passage describing Satan's fall from the Empyrean:)

> "Him the Almighty Power
> Hurled headlong flaming from the ethereal sky,
> With hideous ruin and combustion, down
> To bottomless perdition; there to dwell
> In adamantine chains and penal fire,
> Who durst defy the Omnipotent to arms."

For nine days Satan and his cohorts lay on the fiery lake. But now Satan's fate will involve him in more anger: he is tormented by the thought of lost happiness and lasting pain. He surveys the dismal scene about him, and sees the fallen angel, next to himself in power, Beëlzebub, and addresses him. (Satan's words to Beëlzebub are full of tragic grandeur:)

> "What though the field be lost?
> All is not lost; the unconquerable will,
> And study of revenge, immortal hate,
> And courage never to submit or yield,
> And what is else* not to be overcome?"

[Satan's brilliant mind is a perverted one, and he has forgotten the very nature of Godhead. He has remade God into a being like himself.] He still intends to wage eternal war against God. But Beëlzebub can anticipate nothing but defeat and misery, and sees a future only of pain and eternal punishment. Satan replies that his sole purpose must be to oppose the will of God: if God seeks to bring forth good out of their evil, it must be their business to convert that good into evil.

Satan gazes at the forlorn plain before them, and suggests that they seek rest there from the fiery lake, and hold some consultation as to what is to be done. He rears his mighty form from off the flood, and spreads his wings to fly to dry land (a land that burned with solid, as the lake burned with liquid, fire). Beëlzebub follows him.

Satan surveys Hell. If this place of horrors is to be their home, he hails it as such. In his self-deceiving pride, he exclaims, "Here at least we shall be free!" Beëlzebub now bids him summon the host of fallen angels who are still lying on the burning lake. With irony and spirit Satan arouses them. Abashed they spring up. These fallen angels are later to be worshipped as pagan gods in heathen lands: Moloch, Chemos, Baälim, Ashtaroth, Thammuz,

* i.e., what else is the meaning of not being overcome?

Dagon, Osiris, Isis, Orus, and Belial *; among them there are, too, the classical divine persons: Titan and his offspring, Saturn, Jove, and the rest. As Satan surveys his troops, his heart distends with pride. He addresses them and comforts them with the possibility of their regaining Heaven. He bids them form a council to decide upon the next course of action.

The fallen angels proceed to build a palace, Pandemonium, in the Doric manner. When the edifice is completed, the leaders go far within its recesses to hold their consultation; the others who enter are transformed to a tiny size so that they may all be accommodated in the palace. Within the inner chamber the great council begins.

BOOK TWO

[Satan opens the consultation. The question is whether another attack on Heaven is to be planned.

Fierce Moloch, a military spirit is for immediate and open war against God. Even if the fallen angels lose, what can be worse than to suffer their present lot in Hell?

Attractive-looking Belial speaks next; he pleases the ear but his thoughts are low. Belial recommends peace; after all, despite what Moloch says, things can be much worse than sitting, as we are now doing, in serious consultation. How do we know that God has not worse horrors to unloose on us if we oppose him further? If we had been wise, we should never have warred against God in the first place. If we accept our lot here, we can, at the very worst, accustom ourselves to it.

Mammon carries Belial's argument further. Make the most of our new home, which contains many gems and much gold. Let us possess ourselves of these, and create glorious things out of them here in Hell. Belial's and Mammon's counsel seem to please the hearers.

Beëlzebub, spokesman for Satan, rises now. What is the point of our talking of peace or war? War has undone us, and no peace has been offered by our Conqueror. If we wish to cause Him to reap no joy from His victory, why do we find an easier enterprise? There is a newly created World which God has made for a new race called Man. Though we cannot re-enter Heaven, why should we not attempt either to destroy or to possess that World—or at

---

* Milton invents Belial into a deity. The "sons of Belial" in the Bible simply means "the sons of wickedness."

the least seduce Man to be of our party? This would be the best revenge of all.

This proposal, which is really Satan's, immediately seems like the best one to the leaders, and they vote for it. Satan commends them on their choice. But who will undertake the hazardous voyage through unknown and terrifying Chaos? Who has that much strength and courage?

Satan waits for a reply, but they all sit mute. At length, feeling mighty in his glory, Satan volunteers, accepting the dangers as an honor due to his high place among them.

He leaves on his mission at once lest others, certain to be refused, would now offer to go in his place, and win a reputation cheaply. Upon his departure, the fallen angels (i.e., who now are devils) engage in all sorts of sports—some in games, some in the arts, and some in philosophical discourse.

As Satan approaches Hell's gates, he finds them shut. Guarding them sit Sin and Death. Sin is a woman to the waist, but a serpent from the waist down; around her middle a pack of Hell-hounds run, bark, and, when they wish, creep back into her womb. Death, indistinguishable in form, stands, black as night, shaking a dreadful dart. He strides toward Satan, threatening to strike him; Satan, in turn, aims at him. But Sin rushes between them. Calling Satan "Father," she asks him whether he intends harming his only son. Indignantly he demands to know who she is, why she calls him her sire and that hideous phantasm his son. Sin reminds him how in Heaven, when Satan sat at the head of his assembly conspiring against God, she had suddenly come into being, born in his brain, and thrust out full grown from the left side of his head. Then she was very beautiful, a goddess. Her graces were such as to win the love of Satan (then called Lucifer), and the result of their mating is this horrible son, Death. While he still lay in her womb, she fell from Heaven with the rebel angels, and a key was given into her hands with instructions to keep the gates of Hell locked. Soon she gave birth to Death, whose birth-throes were so terrible that they transformed her lower shape. No sooner born, Death pursued her, forced his embraces upon her, and begot the Hell-hounds in her body. These, in turn, "hourly conceiv'd and hourly born," are an endless torment to her.

Satan now speaks more gently to her, and explains his mission to her. Sin opens the gates of Hell for Satan and he embarks on his perilous journey through Chaos. Sin is unable to shut the doors to Hell which she has opened.

Satan suffers every kind of agony through Chaos, where all atoms are at eternal war with one another. One moment he flies aloft, the next he encounters a vacuum, and falls ten thousand fathoms. His form battered and bruised, the fiend

> O'er bog or steep, through strait, rough, dense, or rare,
> With head, hands, wings, or feet pursues his way,
> And swims, or sinks, or wades, or creeps, or flies,

until he beholds the throne of Chaos.

> The Anarch old
> With falt'ring speech and visage incompos'd

directs Satan to the newly created World.

Satan at last reaches the verge of Chaos. His flight is now easier, as he sees the Empyrean in the distance, "once his native seat," and the created World hanging from there by a golden chain.

BOOK THREE

The scene now changes to the Empyrean.

The opening of this book is one of the most radiant passages in poetry:

> "Hail holy light, offspring of Heaven's first-born . . .
> Bright effluence of bright essence increate . . ."

Milton goes on to speak of what blindness means to him:

> "thee I revisit safe,
> And feel they sovereign vital Lamp; but thou
> Revisit'st not these eyes, that roll in vain
> To find thy piercing ray, and find no dawn; . . .
> . . . Thus with the year
> Seasons return, but not to me returns
> Day, or the sweet approach of even or morn,
> Or sight of vernal bloom, or summer's rose,
> Or flocks or herds, or human face divine;
> But cloud instead, and ever-during dark
> Surrounds me, from the cheerful ways of men
> Cut off . . .
> So much the rather thou celestial light,
> Shine inward, and the mind through all her powers
> Irradiate, there plant eyes, all mist from thence
> Purge and disperse, that I may see and tell
> Of things invisible to mortal sight.

God sitting on his throne, with "the radiant image of His glory," His only Son, sitting at His right hand, sees Satan flying toward the World. God points him out to the Son, and foretells that Satan will succeed in perverting Man and coercing him into transgressing the one command God has laid upon Adam. The fault will be mankind's because Man was created "just and right," able to withstand evil, and free to choose between right and wrong —just as were those angels who fell under the spell of Lucifer. If angel or man had not been created free, what proof could they have given of their allegiance? But since Man will fall because he will be seduced by Satan, God will be merciful to Man; Satan shall not know that mercy because he fell through his own malice.

The Son of God praises the Father for his gracious purposes to Man, and pleads that Man be not finally lost. God replies that Man will continually be disobedient, and Justice will require that Man's posterity must be doomed to destruction unless someone can be found to ransom Man, "death for death." Who among the Heavenly Powers is capable of so much love as to offer himself for that sacrifice?

There is silence in Heaven, and mankind would have been unredeemed had not the Son of God offered himself as the sacrifice.*

> I for his sake will leave
> Thy bosom, and this glory next to thee
> Freely put off, and for him lastly die
> Well pleas'd, on me let Death wreck all his rage.

The Father accepts the Son's offer, ordains the Son's incarnation, and proclaims the Son's exaltation above all names in Heaven and on Earth. He commands all the angels to adore the Son, and they obey, hymning Him to the sound of their harps:

> Thee, Father, first they sung Omnipotent,
> Immutable, Immortal, Infinite,
> Eternal King. . . .
> Thee next they sang of all creation first,
> Begotten Son, Divine Similitude,
> In whose conspicuous count'nance, without cloud
> Made visible, th' Almighty Father shines. . . .

* The Son's offer of self-sacrifice for the redemption of mankind is parallel to Satan's earlier offer to undertake by himself the downfall of mankind.

Meanwhile Satan alights upon the outside of the created World's outermost sphere, the Primum Mobile, on the wall which firmly encloses all the spheres and the Earth at the center.

At first he finds a place called The Limbo of Vanity to which "all things transitory and vain" will hereafter be consigned. Then he comes to the Gate of Heaven, the ladder which Jacob was to see.

Having thus found entry into the World, Satan makes his way from orb to orb to the orb of the Sun. There he finds Uriel, the regent of that sphere. But first he thinks it wise to change his shape to that of a "stripling cherub," with flowing curly locks. Addressing Uriel, he pretends great zeal to see the new creation and especially the new creature Man. Deceived, Uriel praises the false cherub for this desire to witness with his own eyes the new wonders of God. He points out Earth, where Man has his habitation, and the spot on Earth called Paradise, which is Adam's abode. Satan bows in thanks, and speeds his way downward until he lands on the top of Mt. Niphates.*

BOOK FOUR

As Satan views Eden, the home of his destined victims,

> horror and doubt distract
> His troubl'd thoughts, and from the bottom stir
> The Hell within him, for within him Hell
> He brings, and round about him, nor from Hell
> One step no more than from himself can fly
> By change of place.

Conscience awakens despair within him, reminding him of what he was and what he yet must be. He hates the Sun whose beams bring to mind his former glorious state. He cannot pretend that God merited from him anything but praise and thanks for the high place he had been given in Heaven. Yet all of God's goodness provoked only ill and malice in Satan: the lust to raise himself one step higher and be equal to God Himself. He had failed to understand

> that a grateful mind
> By owing owes not, but still pays.

Like all low natures, his was incapable of gratitude. He realizes now what an empty thing is the homage he receives from his

* In a range in Armenia, near Assyria.

fellow-devils, that he is supreme among them only in misery.

He knows that he is doomed by his own nature. Even if God pardoned him, he could never again be reconciled to his old state. He says farewell to hope, fear, and remorse:

> all Good to me is lost;
> Evil be thou my Good.

These evil passions so much disfigure Satan's form that Uriel, who watches Satan from the distance, recognizes him as one of the evil angels. Satan fares onward to the border of Eden, the delicious Paradise of Adam and Eve. It is a garden placed on a plateau whose sides are a thick-grown and steep hill.

In Eden every sort of fruit tree grows, and every sort of blossom and fruit. The very air is pure and delightful. Satan in one bound overleaps the hill and the wall surrounding Eden. He marvels at the beauty he sees. All the creatures he beholds are new to him. But the two who hold him in spell are the noblest of all; they

> Godlike erect, with native Honour clad
> In naked majesty seem'd lords of all,
> And worthy seem'd, for in their looks divine
> The image of their glorious Maker shone.

Adam and Eve pursue their way in the garden, spotlesssly innocent in their nakedness, and feared the sight of neither God nor angel, for their thoughts are free of all ill. They sit down by the side of a stream, after their light toil tending the garden; their appetites and thirsts are wholesome as they begin their supper, made of the luscious fruits of the trees. With the rinds they scoop up water from the brimming stream. They intersperse their supping with smiles and youthful dalliance, as the happy beasts frisk around them.

As the sun begins to decline Satan watches them and feels that he could love them because of their beauty. But all their enviable delights must soon change to woe because of the revenge he must have against God. Hereafter he must dwell with them, he says, or they with him. Regretfully he mixes among the animals in order to begin his villainy, transforming himself from one species to another so that he can get nearer and nearer to his prey. Soon he is close enough to overhear their conversation.

Adam speaks to Eve of the gratitude they both gladly owe to God, who raised them from the dust to enjoy this perfect happiness. In exchange their Maker has asked only that they are

> not to taste that only Tree
> Of Knowledge, planted by the Tree of Life,
> So near grows Death to Life, whate'er Death is.

God has pronounced it death to eat of that forbidden tree. It should be easy to keep that command, since it is

> The only sign of our obedience left
> Among so many signs of power and rule
> Conferr'd upon us.

Eve replies that he has spoken what is right. She recounts her first impressions, after she awakened into consciousness after her creation. A voice led her to the bank of a smooth lake, where she saw her reflection in the water, not knowing that it was the image of herself, and well-pleased with the loveliness her eyes beheld. Then the voice told her that it was her own image, and bade her follow to him who was awaiting her soft embraces. She followed, but, seeing Adam, thought him less fair than her own reflection, and began to run from him. Adam ran after her calling,

> Return, fair Eve,
> Whom fli'st thou? whom thou fli'st, of him thou art,
> His flesh, his bone; to give thee being I lent
> Out of my side to thee, nearest my heart
> Substantial life, to have thee by my side.

With that Adam took her hand, she yielded, and from that time willingly has lived by his direction.

Adam smiles upon Eve as he kisses her. Satan cannot endure the sight of their bliss. Now he speaks with envy of

> these two
> Imparadis't in one another's arms.

They have paradise while he has only Hell. But he has learned something valuable to know: that there is a Tree of Knowledge whose taste is forbidden them. He will teach them to disobey the command. First he must search the garden to find whatever else he may learn.

Uriel now comes to the single entrance to Eden where Gabriel sits chief of the angelic guards, awaiting night. Gabriel, whose task it is to keep strict watch so that no evil thing may enter Eden, is told by Uriel of the latter's encounter with the fallen angel, who for a while deceived him. This devil is now somewhere nearby and Gabriel must find him and expel him.

> Now came still evening on, and twilight gray
> Had in her sober livery all things clad;
> Silence accompanied, for beast and bird,
> They to their grassy couch, these to their nests
> Were slung, all but the wakeful nightingale;
> She all night long her amorous descant sung;
> Silence was pleased.

Adam and Eve walk hand and hand to their bower of bliss, adore God in a hymn, and begin to enjoy the holy pleasures of married love. [Milton denies that sexual love came into existence as a result of Adam's fall and inveighs against those hypocrites who, talking of innocence and purity, defame

> as impure what God declares
> Pure, and commands to some, leaves free to all.
> Our Maker bids increase, who bids abstain
> But our destroyer, foe to God and man?

And here the poet sings his own hymn to wedded Love.]

Gabriel now sends his guardian troops to scour Eden to find Satan and expel him. Ithuriel's troop heads for the bower where Adam and Eve are lying in sleep, and there they find Satan squat like a toad at the ear of Eve. Ithuriel touches him lightly with his spear, and Satan is forced to start up in his own shape.

When questioned as to his identity, Satan proudly and sneeringly reminds them that they all have good reason to know Lucifer, who was once matchless in Heaven. Zephon, answering scorn with scorn, assures him that since his revolt he no longer has the beauty and radiance he once wore in the Empyrean. Realizing himself powerless against these emissaries of Goodness, Satan accompanies the band to where Gabriel is posted. Gabriel asks him why he has broken his bounds of Hell, and Satan mockingly replies, "Who is in love with his pain? Let God bar His iron gates more firmly." Gabriel denounces him as a hypocrite masquerading as a patron of liberty, and asks him to remember how useless resistance will be. The Fiend, seeing the scales of Justice decided against him, flees murmuring to himself in rage.

BOOK FIVE

It is morning. Adam finds Eve still sleeping in unquiet slumber, and awakens her. She tells him that she has had such a dream as she never had before: close at her ear someone summoned her to walk forth; she rose, and thinking it had been Adam who had called her, went to find him; suddenly she was at the Tree of Knowledge, which in the night seemed even fairer than by day; beside it stood a winged figure like an angel, who plucked and tasted the forbidden fruit; she was horrified, but the bold angel offered her the fruit and bade her taste it so that she might become a goddess; she could not resist the savory odor and ate; at once she flew up into the air with her guide and beheld the earth beneath her—when at once her tempter was gone, and she was on the ground again asleep. She is relieved to be awake.

Adam comforts her with the assurance that wicked ideas in the mind, when one disapproves of having had them, leave one blameless. They come forth to their day's labor, the tending of plants in their garden, and sing a hymn of praise to God.

In order to give Man all the knowledge he needs to resist Satan, God sends down Raphael to warn Adam. Raphael comes to Eden, is greeted by Adam, and is entertained by Eve and her spouse with their choicest fruits.

Raphael delivers his message, warning Adam of his enemy:

> That thou are happy, owe to God;
> That thou continu'st such, owe to thyself,
> That is, to thy obedience; therein stand. . . .
> God made thee perfect, not immutable;
> And good he made thee, but to preserve
> He left in thy power, ordain'd thy will
> By nature free, not over-rul'd by Fate
> Inextricable, or strict necessity.

At Adam's request Raphael enlarges upon Satan's history. [The reader is brought in this way to the actual beginning of the story of the epic with Raphael's account of how Lucifer was first moved by envy to gather a third of the angels in Heaven under his leadership, and incited them to rebel against God.] Out of malice against the Son of God, Lucifer summoned the angelic powers under his command and stirred them to resentment. It was irksome enough, he said, to pay homage to the Father, but too much to pay the tribute of subservience to the Son now as well. But Abdiel, an angel loyal to God, stood up and upbraided Lucifer for his blasphemous argument, but no one seconded his objections. Exulting in his success, Lucifer went on to deny Abdiel's reminder that the angels were the creation of God. Who saw this creation when it was a-making? How do we know that we are not self-begotten? Lucifer sarcastically urged Abdiel to run and carry the tale of the incipient rebellion to the Almighty

Throne before harm befall him from his own comrades. Undismayed at standing alone in that crew, Abdiel continued his defiance of their evil designs and quit their company.

BOOK SIX

Raphael continues his narrative about the revolt in Heaven. Michael and Gabriel were sent forth to battle against Lucifer, who is now known as Satan (the Adversary). After the first fight Satan and his cohorts were forced to retire. Satan called a council, and the devils invented hideous implements of destruction, and in the second day's fight caused great confusion among Michael's ranks. But the loyal angels pulled up mountains and with them overwhelmed Satan's forces. On the third day God sent his Son to crush the rebellion. Driving into the midst of the enemy, the Son pursued them to the wall of Heaven, which now opened; and Satan's troops fell down into the vast abyss of Chaos. They fell for nine days until they reached the shores of Hell, which had been prepared to receive them. The Messiah turned his triumphal chariot about and was jubilantly greeted by all the loyal host of Heaven.

At this point Raphael reminds Adam that Satan envies him his happy state, and is now plotting to seduce him from obedience to God so that Man may partake of the rebel angel's misery.

> But list'n not to his temptations, warn
> Thy weaker;* let it profit thee to have heard
> By terrible example the reward
> Of disobedience; firm they might have stood.
> Yet fell; remember, and fear to transgress.

BOOK SEVEN

Raphael continues his narrative. At Adam's request he relates how the new Universe was created because God had desired to fill up the ranks of the lost angels with a new creature, Man. God sent His Son to create in six days the wonders of the Universe.

But first the poet opens with a new invocation to Urania, in which he refers to the moral debasement of the Restoration (the period in which he is now composing his poem):

> On evil days though fall'n, and evil tongues;

and speaks of the blindness in which his inspiration must thrive and of his hopes to find a "fit audience . . . though few."

* i.e., Eve.

Before beginning his new account, Raphael remarks that he has been instructed to answer Adam's "desire of knowledge within bounds." But Adam is not to lust after knowing the unknowable, those mysteries

> which th' invisible King,
> Only Omniscient, hath supprest in Night,
> To none communicable in Earth or Heaven.
> Enough is left besides to search and know.

God created the race of Man, who shall dwell on Earth until, by Man's proof of obedience, that race should be prepared to live in Heaven. (Thus Adam, by his fall, will frustrate God's plan of having mankind develop into beings like the angels.) God sent forth his Son to create the new World (i.e., Universe).

Raphael continues to recount, in a magnificent elaboration of *Genesis* I (with an occasional inspiration from *Genesis* II), the Creation as it took place on six successive days. There is a beautiful detailing of the fishes, birds, and animals which come into being. When Creation is completed, a great hymn is sung in Heaven on the seventh day, containing the noble thought:

> to create
> Is greater than created to destroy.*

> *For what can War, but endless War still breed,*
> *Till Truth and Right from Violence be freed?*

and the sonnet to Cromwell (1652):

> *peace hath her victories*
> *No less renown'd than war.*

In the second edition of *Paradise Lost* (1674) Book VII was divided into two books at line 640; for this new arrangement the first four lines of Book VIII were added by Milton.

BOOK EIGHT

Adam now inquires about the motions of the Heavenly bodies. Since her spouse seems about to enter into an abstruse discussion, Eve rises and goes forth among her fruits and flowers to take care of them. It is not that she is incapable of listening to exalted talk, but that she prefers to wait to hear such exalted conceptions from Adam's lips, since he will intermix conjugal caresses with his information:

* Cf. the sonnet to Gen. Fairfax (1648):

from his lip
Not words alone pleased her.

Raphael approves Adam's desire to know, and gives him much information, but he also warns him:

Heav'n is for thee too high
To know what passes there; be lowly wise:
Think only what concerns thee and thy being.

The archangel now expresses a desire to hear Adam's own story. In a wonderful narrative Adam describes the beginning of his own consciousness after his creation. He was lying on the ground when,

Straight toward Heav'n my wondering eyes I turn'd,
And gaz'd a while the ample sky, till rais'd
By quick instinctive motion up I sprung,
As thitherward endeavoring, and upright
Stood on my feet.

He looked at the world about him, found he could speak, and at once began to speak in praise of the sun and the splendors of the creation which his eyes beheld. Then One came, to lead him to the Paradise of Eden which awaited him. Rejoicing at the wonders he saw, Adam fell in adoration at the feet of his Guide. He raised Adam up and told him that all was for Adam to keep and care for. Adam was to be free to eat of every tree growing in the garden but that of the Tree of the Knowledge of Good and Evil,

which I have set
The pledge of thy obedience and thy faith.

Let Adam never forget:

The day thou eat'st thereof, my sole command
Transgrest, inevitably thou shalt die,
From that day mortal, and this happy state
Shalt lose, expell'd from hence into a world
Of woe and sorrow.

Adam says he never can forget the severity with which that penalty was promised; but he knows too that it is in his own power never to incur it.

Returning to His mild voice, God now brought the animals to Adam to be named, and Adam named them, as they came to him in pairs. But Adam was thus made to realize his own solitariness, having, unlike the animals, no partner for himself. Pleased with Adam's plea for a mate, God put Adam's body to sleep, although Adam's inner sight was able to perceive what was happening. God stooped, opened Adam's left side, took out a rib, and with His hands God fashioned the loveliest of all creatures. When Adam awaked, he saw her being led to him by his Guide. Adam cried out his thanks to the Maker for giving him Woman, the best of all His gifts. Then Adam led her to their nuptial bower, the Heavens, the stars, the Earth, the birds—even the air— gave approval, and all night long the nightingale sang a marriage-song for them.

Adam realizes that though Eve has been created inferior to him in intellect, yet she is so perfect and complete in her loveliness

> that what she wills to do or say
> Seems wisest, virtuousest, discreetest, best.

Raphael admonishes Adam that though he does well to honor, love, and cherish Woman, he must remain her head.

> In loving thou dost well, in passion not,
> Wherein true love consists not.

He is to distinguish between true conjugal love, which is friendly to reason, and carnal pleasure, which reduces man to the beasts.

With another warning to Adam against Satan,

> Be strong, live happy, and love, but first of all
> Him whom to love is to obey, and keep
> His great command; take heed lest passion sway
> Thy judgment to do aught, which else free will
> Would not admit.

Raphael is thanked by Adam, and departs.

BOOK NINE (the longest book in *Paradise Lost*)

Approaching the climax of his story, Milton announces the change of tone to the tragic, for now he must speak no longer of Man conversing with God or Angel-guest, but of

> foul distrust, and breach
> Disloyal on the part of Man, revolt,
> And disobedience;

and on the part of Heaven, now alienated,

> distance and distaste,
> Anger and just rebuke, and judgment giv'n,
> That brought into this World a world of woe,
> Sin and her shadow Death, and Misery,
> Death's harbinger.

This, nevertheless, is a subject more heroic than those of the *Iliad, Odyssey,* or *Aeneid.* The poet invokes the aid of Urania, who grants him inspiration and dictates the lines to him at night as he lies in his bed.

At night Satan returns to Eden in the form of a mist. He finds a serpent sleeping and decides this creature to be the fittest for him to enter. Before doing so Satan has a powerfully bitter soliloquy. He hymns the beauties and wonders of Earth, and marvels at Man, who sums up all that earthly creation has to offer. How willingly would Satan reside here if he could find joy in anything! But the more he sees pleasures about him, the more he feels torment within. He knows that what he now seeks will make himself no less miserable: all he can hope is to make others as miserable as himself, even though worse misery accrue to himself from the deed.

> But what will not ambition and revenge
> Descend to? Who aspires must down as low
> As high he soar'd, obnoxious* first or last
> To basest things. Revenge, at first though sweet,
> Bitter ere long back on itself recoils.
> Let it.

Satan enters the body of the sleeping serpent.

Morning comes, and Adam and Eve awake. Eve suggests that they could accomplish more if they separate during the day, each to do his own labors in the garden. When they are together, the sight of each other causes them to interrupt their work with endearing talk; they will accomplish more if each goes his own way for the day. Adam approves Eve's desire to accomplish more, yet he finds no harm in their working leisurely and enjoying each other's company. However, he agrees to try the experiment. But one thing disturbs him: she is aware of the malicious foe who intends to assault them; will it not be easier for Satan to attack them singly? Are they not safer together?

* exposed to harm from.

> The Wife, where danger or dishonor lurks,
> Safest and seemliest by her Husband stays,
> Who guards her, or with her the worst endures.

Eve is hurt that Adam should doubt her firmness to God or him.
Adam apparently fears, she says, that her faith and love are so
weak that they can easily be shaken by anyone else. How could
Adam think such thoughts of one who loves him so well?

Adam replies that he does not doubt her; he himself would
feel stronger against their foe if she remains by his side. Why
doesn't she feel the same?

But Eve responds: are we to be confined in our movements
because of this foe? How is either of us to prove his faith, love,
and virtue unless they are tested without help from the other?
Our happiness is frail indeed if we are to live hereafter in con-
stant fear of this foe.

Adam is forced to admit that Man can receive no harm
against his own free will, for Man has reason to protect him.
Still, it is better not to go looking for trouble:

> Trial will come unsought.
> Wouldst thou approve thy constancy, approve
> First thy obedience.

Nevertheless, since she is so anxious to leave his side, let her go,

> for thy stay, not free, absents thee more.

Eve goes, insisting that it is with his permission. Moreover,
their proud foe will not seek to attack the weaker. He is bound
to prefer tempting Adam. Eve goes her own path, urged by
Adam to return soon.

Satan, in the body of the serpent, searches for the pair, not
daring to hope to find Eve alone, but so he finds her. He draws
closer and closer to her, sometimes seen, sometimes hidden. He
is so enchanted with the beauty both of her and the place, that
for a time he remains "stupidly good," disarmed of his enmity
and revenge. But he recollects his mission, and makes his way
to Eve

> on his rear,
> Circular base of rising folds, that tour'd
> Fold above fold a surging maze,

for the serpent in those days was not yet "prone on the ground."

Satan fawns upon Eve, and licks the ground where she walks

until he procures her astonished attention. He begins to speak in the most flattering terms, extolling her over all other creatures. She ought to be, he concludes, a "goddess among gods," served adoringly by the angels themselves.

Eve is amazed that the serpent can talk in the language of Man, and asks how a creature she thought dumb has come by such understanding. The serpent replies that the fruit of a certain tree in the Garden has given him speech and reason. Eve asks to be brought to the tree. The serpent leads her to the Tree of the Knowledge of Good and Evil. When she sees which tree it is, she assures him that he has gone to needless trouble, since

> of this Tree we may not taste nor touch.

Pretending to be incensed at the injustice to Man in this prohibition, the serpent promises Eve that the fruit of this tree will give her not Death but Life. Is he not himself very much alive as a consequence of having eaten of it? Moreover, though God has threatened her if she disobey the injunction, how could he be a just God to punish her for such a petty trespass? And if He is not just, how can He be God? And if He is not God, why need He be obeyed? Obviously the prohibition was only to keep Man low and ignorant: He knows that on the day Adam and Eve eat of this fruit they will become as gods. Finally, if God owns everything, how can the tree impart anything which would be against His will?

These sophistries weaken Eve's objections. She is hungry, and the fruit smells delicious. She reflects: this fruit must indeed be wonderful if it can make the brute intelligent; God apparently forbids Man to be wise in wishing to deprive him of this knowledge of Good and Evil; moreover, the serpent has not died, though Death was the promised punishment; why should she not now feed "both body and mind?"

Eve eats of the fruit and is pleased with the taste. The serpent, meanwhile, slinks away, forgotten by Eve. She is so delighted with this Tree that she promises to make it her special care. Already she sees herself one with the gods. Perhaps God has not seen her—Heaven is so far away. But what shall she say to Adam? Shall she allow her spouse to share in the new blessings of this fruit or shall she keep the knowledge to herself and maintain superiority over him by eating of it secretly? But suppose God *has* seen what she has done? She then would die and Adam

would be wedded to another woman—a thought she cannot
bear.

> So dear I love him, that with him all deaths
> I could endure.

Adam, who, eager for her return, has woven a garland of
flowers for her, feels suddenly an uneasiness for her, and goes to
seek her. He finds her by the Tree of Knowledge, a bough of its
fruit in her hand. She tells how she has missed him, and that she
will never again leave his side. She then admits having eaten of
the forbidden fruit, explains her reasons, announces that her
heart and mind seem already to have expanded, and assures
Adam that she has performed the forbidden experiment all for
his sake. He must now eat of the fruit too, lest she become
divine and be forced to be separated from him.

Adam, overwhelmed with dismay at her sin, and certain that
she will now die, is unable to face the prospect of losing her.
Knowing that he too must be lost, conscious that he is sinning, he
also eats of the fruit.

> He scrupl'd not to eat
> Against his better knowledge, not deceiv'd,
> But fondly overcome with female charm.

Earth trembles and Nature groans at his act, and there is a
distant peal of thunder.

The first reaction in Adam and Eve is a kind of drunken ex-
citement. They both exult in their trespass. Adam, burning
with lust, compliments Eve in having discovered new pleasures.
If forbidden joys are as good as this one, what a pity that ten
trees had not been prohibited to them instead of only one! He
leads her, quite willing, to their bower for an amorous bout,
for the first time incited by lust, not love. At length, weary, they
fall asleep.

When they awake, they rise "as from unrest," unrefreshed,
their innocence gone. Adam now upbraids Eve for what she
has done. How is he to face God or angel again? Ashamed of
their nakedness now, they seek covering for it, and find it in
leaves of the banyan tree. Anger, hate, mistrust, and suspicion
arise in their minds for the first time, and Adam blames his
wife for insisting on going off by herself that morning. She
replies: how does he know that he might not have yielded to
the serpent's suggestions too if he had been there? Besides, why

did he not forbid her going? If anything he seemed anxious to dismiss her then.

> Thus they in mutual accusation spent
> The fruitless hours, but neither self-condemning.*

BOOK TEN

Man's sin is known in Heaven. The angels who have been guarding Eden return to Heaven, unable to account for the success of Satan. God exonerates them of all blame: they could not have prevented Satan's invasion of the Earthly Paradise. God sends His Son to judge Adam and Eve.

The Son curses the serpent and dooms it to grovel on its belly henceforth and eat of the dust all the days of its life: there shall be eternal enmity between Man and the serpent. The judgment upon Eve is that Woman will bring forth her offspring in sorrow, and be in subjection to her husband. The judgment upon Adam is that Man shall eat in sorrow all his days, that the ground shall bring forth weeds and thorns, that Man shall eat in the sweat of his face, and eventually die, returning as dust to dust.

In the meantime, Sin and Death, waiting at the Gates of Hell, are aware of Satan's victory over Man, and decide to follow their father up to Man's universe. To make the way easier from Hell, they pave a broad highway over Chaos. They meet Satan and congratulate him. He returns to Pandemonium, where he relates his success. When his audience would applaud, the fallen angels are all turned into serpents who can only hiss.

In the Empyrean, God promises the eventual and final victory of His Son over the devils, Sin, and Death. For the present God commands his angels to make several alterations in the Heavens and the Elements, for Nature is no longer pure. The Sun is ordained to so move and shine as to affect the Earth with severe heat and cold; winter and intense summer come into being. The winds are assigned their quarters so as to afflict sea, air and shore; the thunder has its work appointed. Vapors, mists, and hot exhalations, ice, snow, and hail, storms in forest and on the seas—all these begin their careers. Beasts, fowl, and fish now begin to prey upon one another.

---

* Later, unlike Satan, both Adam and Eve are each willing to assume the entire responsibility for their sin. When they achieve that position, they are on the way to earning eventual forgiveness for the race.

Adam, seeing the changes which have come upon the face of the earth, laments:

> Is this the end
> Of this new glorious World?

Yet he cannot conceal from himself that he is the author of his own misery. He could bear his punishment, but the thought that his posterity must share the punishment is unbearable.

Eve, seeing his affliction, tries to console him: she is more unhappy over his condition than her own.

He harshly repels her, "Out of my sight, thou serpent!" and bitterly reflects on the miserable lot of men in having to co-exist with the falsity and weakness of women.

She pleads with him not to forsake her. Her fate is worse than his: he has sinned against God, but she has sinned against God and him. She will plead with God to visit punishment on her head alone,

> On me, sole cause to thee of all this woe.

She weeps from the bottom of her wretchedness.

Adam, moved by her tears and her ability to accept full responsibility for their joint wrong, loses his anger and comforts her. If prayers could alter God's decrees, he would speed before her to demand that he alone be punished. (Thus, facing their guilt, both are on the road to redemption.)

Eve, still wild with grief, now suggests that to avoid passing on the curse to future generations, they either refrain from mating henceforth and die childless, or else put an end to themselves and thus cheat Death of future prey. Adam rejects both plans. He reminds her that the Son's judgment was mild in comparison with what they had reason to expect. He is not afraid of the labor now imposed upon him. It will be better to prostrate themselves before God, admit their faults, beg for forgiveness with sincere sorrow, and submit themselves to God's will.

And this they both proceed to do. Adam has also reminded her that the Son promised in His judgment, that her seed should be revenged upon the serpent.

BOOK ELEVEN

The Son of God presents the prayers of Adam and Eve to the Father. God accepts His Son's intercession, but declares that they can no longer live in Eden. Michael is sent down with a band of cherubim to dispossess them. He is also commanded to give Adam a view of the future of his race.

Refreshed after their prayers, Adam has an intuition of further changes in store for them. He sees the approach of the angels, and is prepared for a new order of life to be ordained for them. Adam goes to meet Michael.

The Angel announces that they must leave Eden. Eve weeps bitterly, while Adam is struck dumb with grief. To her leaving Eden is worse than Death. Michael reminds her that she must submit, and that, after all, she will not be alone. Adam is more concerned that, leaving Eden, he will no longer be granted conference with God and the angels. Michael recalls to him that God is not only in Eden, but everywhere. Adam ceases his complaints.

Michael now leads Adam up to a high hill and sets before him in vision a series of events in the history of his offspring, up to the time of the Flood. The purpose of this is to remind him that God is abiding, and that Man must learn submissiveness to the Divine Will. [This passage and its continuation in most of Book XII are a marvelous summary of chief events in the Old Testament.]

In the second edition of *Paradise Lost* the original *Book X* was divided into two books. The first five lines of *Book XII* were added by Milton in 1674 to open the last book.

BOOK TWELVE

Michael's vision continues with events after the Flood, through Abraham, and the Incarnation, Death, and Resurrection of the Savior. Moses and Joshua are seen as types of the Christ. Adam is satisfied that his race will be eventually redeemed, and understands Man's place in the Redemption. He is determined to learn patience, obedience, and self-restraint. Michael congratulates him:

> This having learnt, thou hast attained the sum
> Of wisdom.

They descend the hill.

Eve, in the meantime, in her sleep, has had dreams which have composed her mind to submission. Michael takes Adam and Eve each by the hand, and leads them out of Eden. When they look back they see a fiery sword and ranks of cherubim guarding the entrance to Eden.

The concluding lines are as triumphantly beautiful as anything in the poem:

> In either hand the hastening Angel caught
> Our lingering parents, and to the Eastern Gate
> Led them direct, and down the cliff as fast
> To the subjected plain; then disappeared.
> They looking back, all the Eastern side beheld
> Of Paradise, so late their happy seat,
> Waved over by that flaming brand, the Gate
> With dreadful faces thronged and fiery arms.
> Some natural tears they dropped, but wiped them soon;
> The world was all before them, where to choose
> Their place of rest, and Providence their guide.
> They, hand in hand, with wandering steps and slow,
> Through Eden took their solitary way.

Last Works

Near the end of 1665 Thomas Ellwood in returning the manuscript of *Paradise Lost* said to Milton, "Thou hast said much of Paradise lost, but what has thou to say of Paradise found?" When he visited the poet again in 1666 Milton showed him a new poem, and said, "This is owing to you; for you put it in my head by the question you put to me at Chalfont." Despite Ellwood's claim for credit in the birth of *Paradise Regained,* it is more likely that Milton had planned this work for some time. In *The Reason of Church Government* he had speculated as to whether he ought to write his great poem as a long epic in the style of Homer and Virgil, a short epic in the style of *Job,* or as an Aristotelian tragedy. *Paradise Lost* was written in the manner of the first kind; *Paradise Regained* in the manner of the second; *Samson Agonistes* in the manner of the third.

Paradise Regained is, moreover, in logical sequence to its predecessor. Its theme is "one man's firm obedience fully tried through all temptation." It depicts Jesus' coming into a realization of his mission on earth; it is an attempt to explore the mystery of His "superhumanity." It was natural that Milton should find an analogy in his poem first between Jesus and Hercules, hero of incorruptible integrity and giant strength, and secondly between Jesus and Socrates, the pre-eminent man of ancient Greece.

The poem is amazing for its fluent learning, its historical perspective, its epitomizing the knowledge of the ancient world, its description of Rome of the Caesars.

Paradise Regained

Written 1665-67, *Paradise Regained* was published in 1671 together with *Samson Agonistes.* In it we find man's lost Paradise regained through the victory of Christ over Satan, the victory foretold of Eve's seed over the serpent. The poem deals with the period in Christ's life immediately following His baptism by John and preceding His ministry in the world.

Like the *Book of Job* this short epic has passages chiefly of dialogue with short connecting narrative sections. The blank verse is austere and pared to the naked essentials of the meaning. The four books deal with Satan's three efforts at tempting Christ in the order recounted in *Luke,* Chapter 4.

BOOK ONE

The opening lines connect this work with *Paradise Lost.* Christ's thwarting of Satan parallels Adam's failure.

Satan hears God's announcement at Jesus' baptism that "This is My beloved Son." Satan at once calls another council of devils in mid-air, and undertakes the new mission of seducing Jesus.

In Heaven God foretells that Jesus, the new Adam, will emerge victorious.

Jesus, after baptism at Jordan, is led by the Holy Spirit into the wilderness. For forty days he has nothing to eat. It is then that Satan approaches him in the guise of an old man, and bids him, if he is indeed the Son of God, to convert a stone into bread to satisfy his hunger. Jesus overcomes this first temptation by observing that man does not live by bread alone. It is not his purpose to change the natural order of things.

Satan, exposed as himself, fawns on Jesus and utters a sophistical complaint, which Jesus repulses. Christ tells him he has earned his present wretchedness. Satan vanishes, and night is ushered in.

BOOK TWO

Andrew and Simon, and others not named in Holy Writ, are worried about the disappearance of Jesus, but find relief in the belief that God will fulfill his promises. Mary, too, seeing many returning from the baptism but not her son, is concerned; but she has learned to be patient.

Satan returns to his band in the middle-air. Belial suggests tempting Jesus with the lure of women, but Satan knows that the sort of expedient which undid Adam would be of no avail with Jesus. Instead he suggests honor and popular acclaim as the means of a new temptation: Satan will offer Christ the kingdoms of the world and their glory.

Christ must be in hunger after his long fast. Satan comes to him to ask whether he would now not eat if food were set before him. That would depend, Christ answers, upon the giver. A rich Roman banquet is the first part of the temptation, but Jesus rejects that.

Next Satan offers Jesus worldly riches, a sure help to earthly power, but Jesus repudiates wealth when unaccompanied by righteousness. Worldly dominion purchased by riches is meaningless.

> Yet he who reigns within himself, and rules
> Passions, desires, and fears, is more a king.

BOOK THREE

This second temptation is continued with Satan's offer of the most insidious of worldly temptations, glory. Christ scorns the glory that comes to conquerors. The only true glory is that of the spirit, won by men who never thought of worldly fame.

Satan now attempts a more personal attraction for Jesus, the fulfillment of his ministry on earth. Showing Jesus the kingdoms of the earth, he offers to put them all under Jesus, if Jesus will worship him. Jesus replies that the time for his dominion over the world is not yet. The deliverance of Israel from bondage is in God's power, not his own.

BOOK FOUR

Satan bids Jesus look west, and see how Rome, mistress of the world, is in Satan's dominion. All this pride and grandeur can be Jesus', if he will fall down and worship Satan. Jesus rejects this offer.

As his final essay in the temptation of glory, Satan proposes the splendors of intellectual accomplishment, seen at its best in old Athens. But great though this temptation is, Jesus resolves all these offers of worldly glory by saying disdainfully, "Get thee behind me, Satan." Jesus can worship God alone.

Satan now brings Jesus to Jerusalem and sets him on a pinnacle of the Temple, for the third of the three temptations. If Jesus be indeed the Son of God he can test it by casting himself down, assured that God will not allow him to be hurt. But Jesus repels this last temptation, perfect as he is in his faith, and therefore unwilling to tempt God.

Satan is forced to recognize Jesus' invincibility, and disappears. Jesus stands safely on the pinnacle. A band of angels ease him from his station, and bear him to the valley, where all manner of food and drink is set before him.

Unobserved, Jesus quietly returns to the house of his mother.

Paradise Regained, because it is less dramatic and more severe, has been less read than *Paradise Lost,* but it was Wordsworth's favorite. It has a quieter, but a no less powerful, tone. And Milton's summary of the civilizations of the world and the learning of Greece are among the most notable examples of his erudition applied to the purposes of great poetry.

Samson Agonistes

Milton's last great work, written 1668-70, was published with *Paradise Regained* in 1671. It is the culminating work of Milton's career, and exhibits his style at its greatest elevation of austerity. Not a word could be spared, there is no decoration, and the poetry has the massiveness of bronze. For his last work Milton employed the form of Greek tragedy, especially as practiced by the greatest of Greek dramatists, Sophocles. In fact the very situation of the play and certain of its events remind one of Sophocles' *Oedipus at Colonus.*

Like all Greek tragedies, there is in this work a basic conception of five acts. The first act terminates at line 325 and contains Samson's soliloquy and discourse to the Chorus. The second act ends at line 710 and contains the Manoa episode. The third act ends at line 1060 and contains the Delilah episode. The fourth act terminates at line 1440 and contains the episodes of Harapha and the Officer. The fifth act deals with Manoa's reappearance and the announcement of the catastrophe.

The story is concerned with the last day in the life of the great Hebrew hero Samson. (Milton's source is *Judges,* 13-16). We find Samson blind and captive, working for the Philistines in their city of Gaza. It is a festival day, and he is released for the day from his heavy labors. He comes forth into the open air and bemoans his condition. He receives a visit of certain friends of his people (constituting the Chorus) who comfort him as well as they can. Then his old father, Manoa, comes to see him and announces his intention of trying to win Samson's freedom by paying a ransom. It is a matter of anguish to both father and son that the Philistines on this day are celebrating in thanksgiving for their deliverance from Samson. After Manoa departs to sue to the Philistian lords for his son's liberty, Delilah, Samson's wife, a daughter of the Philistines, comes to see her husband. Delilah attempts to win Samson's forgiveness for her act of treachery in delivering him to the hands of his enemies. Her excuse is that out of love for Samson she wanted to keep him with her in her own country. He rejects her deceptive wiles, and in a fit of wrath she reveals herself for the traitress that she really is. Next comes Harapha, the athlete, a bully who insults Samson now that he is blind and apparently without strength. A public officer arrives to summon Samson to appear before the lords at their feast in an exhibition of his strength. He at first refuses. But suddenly, inwardly persuaded that God desires him to go, he consents to accompany the officer on the latter's reappearance. To the Chorus Manoa returns with great hope that he can procure his son's deliverance. In the midst of his account, a messenger comes to relate how Samson has sacrificed his life for God, in pulling down the roof on the heads of the Philistian assembly. He and all present lost their lives. But in his death he has regained God's favor.

It is impossible to escape the conviction that Milton to a certain extent was writing about himself in *Samson Agonistes*. Like Samson, he was living blind and alone among his enemies (the period of the Restoration); like Samson, he had taken to wife a daughter of the enemy (his first wife, of Cavalier family); like Samson, he placed his trust in God to justify his beliefs. The play thus becomes one more assertion of Milton's unquenchable spirit of integrity. But there is a very special pathos that readers of the play will feel. For in Samson's mouth Milton at last speaks to us of the horrors of blindness.

SELECTED BIBLIOGRAPHY

Adams, R. M. *Ikon*, Cornell University Press, 1955

Addison, J. *Criticism on Milton's Paradise Lost*, A. Murray & Son, 1868

Agar, H. *Milton and Plato*, Princeton University Press, 1928

Allen, D. C. *The Harmonious Vision*, Johns Hopkins Press, 1954

Arthos, J. *On A Mask Presented at Ludlow Castle*, University of Michigan Press, 1954

Bailey, J. C. *Milton*, T. Butterworth, 1932

Banks, T. H. *Milton's Imagery*, Columbia University Press, 1950

Barker, A. E. *Milton and the Puritan Dilemma*, University of Toronto Press, 1942

Belloc, Hillaire. *Milton*, J. B. Lippincott Co., 1935

Bowra, C. M. *From Virgil to Milton*, Macmillan & Co. Ltd., 1948

Bradshaw, J. *A Concordance to the Poetical Works of John Milton*, The Macmillan Co., 1894

Bridges, Robert. *Milton's Prosody*, Oxford University Press, 1921

Broadbent, J. B. *Comus and Samson Agonistes: Milton*. ("Barron's Studies in English Literature Series," ed. David Daiches.) Barron's Educational Series, 1963

Brown, E. G. *Milton's Blindness*, Columbia University Press, 1938

Bush, D. *Paradise Lost in Our Time*, Cornell University Press, 1945; *The Renaissance and English Humanism*, University of Toronto Press, 1939

Buxton, C. R. *Prophets of Heaven and Hell*, Cambridge University Press, 1945

Cawley, R. R. *Milton's Literary Craftsmanship*, Oxford University Press, 1941; *Milton and the Literature of Travel*, Princeton University Press, 1951

Clark, D. L. *John Milton at St. Paul's School*, Columbia University Press, 1948

Coleridge, S. T. *Lectures on Shakespeare etc.*, E. P. Dutton & Co., 1951

Conklin, G. N. *Biblical Criticism and Heresy in Milton*, King's Crown Press, 1949

Cooper, Lane. *A Concordance of the Latin, Greek and Italian Poems of John Milton*, Halle, Niemeyer, 1923

Corcoran, M. I. *Milton's Paradise Lost with Reference to the Hexameral Background*, Catholic University of America Press, 1945

Darbishire, H. *The Early Lives of Milton*, Constable & Co. Ltd., 1932

De Selincourt, E. *English Poets and the National Ideal*, Oxford University Press, 1916

Diekhoff, J. S. (ed.) *Milton on Himself,* Oxford University Press, 1939; *Milton's Paradise Lost,* Columbia University Press, 1946

Dorian, D. C. *The English Diodatis,* Rutgers University Press, 1950

Fletcher, H. F. *The Intellectual Development of John Milton,* University of Illinois Press, 1956; *The Use of the Bible in Milton's Prose,* University of Illinois Press, 1929; *Milton's Rabbinical Readings,* University of Illinois Press, 1930

French, J. M. *Milton in Chancery,* Modern Language Association, 1939

Gilbert, A. H. *On the Composition of Paradise Lost,* University of North Carolina Press, 1947

Grierson, H. J. C. *Criticism and Creation,* Chatto & Windus, 1949; *Milton and Wordsworth,* Cambridge University Press, 1937

Gurteen, S. H. *The Epic of the Fall of Man,* G. P. Putnam's Sons, 1896

Hanford, J. H. *The Youth of Milton,* University of Michigan Press, 1925; *A Milton Handbook,* F. S. Crofts & Co., 1939; *John Milton, Englishman,* Gollancz, 1950

Harding, D. P. *Milton and the Renaissance Ovid,* University of Illinois Press, 1946

Harrison, T. P. *They Tell of Birds,* University of Texas Press, 1956

Hartwell, K. E. *Lactantius and Milton,* Harvard University Press, 1929

Havens, R. H. *The Influence of Milton on English Poetry,* Harvard University Press, 1922

Hutchinson, F. E. *Milton and the English Mind,* Hodder & Stoughton, 1946

Johnson, Samuel. *Lives of the Poets,* Edited by G. B. Hill, Oxford University Press, 1905

Kelley, M. *This Great Argument,* Princeton University Press, 1941

Kennedy, M. S. *John Milton and His Minor Poems,* Vermont Printing Co., 1922

Kirkonnell, W. *The Celestial Cycle,* University of Toronto Press, 1952

Knight, G. W. *Chariot of Wrath,* Faber & Faber, 1942

Krouse, F. M. *Milton's Samson and the Christian Tradition,* Princeton University Press, 1949

Langdon, I. *Milton's Theory of Poetry and Fine Art,* Yale University Press, 1924

Larson, M. A. *The Modernity of Milton,* University of Chicago Press, 1927

Le Comte, E. S. *Yet Once More,* Liberal Arts Press, 1953

Lewis, C. S. *A Preface to Paradise Lost,* Oxford University Press, 1943

Liljegren, S. B. *Studies in Milton,* Lund Publishing Co., 1918

McColley, G. *Paradise Lost,* Packard & Co., 1940

Macaulay, R. *Milton,* Harper & Bros., 1935

Masson, D. *The Life of John Milton, Narrated in Connexion with the Political, Ecclesiastical, and Literary History of His Time,* The Macmillan Co., 1859-94

Masterman, J. H. B. *The Age of Milton,* G. Bell & Sons, 1904

Maurice, F. D. *The Friendship of Books*, Macmillan & Co. Ltd., 1880

Mohl, R. *Studies in Spenser, Milton and the Theory of Monarchy*, King's Crown Press, 1949

Muir, K. *John Milton*, Longmans, Green & Co., 1955

Osgood, C. G. *The Classical Mythology of Milton's English Poems*, Oxford University Press, 1925

Parker, W. R. *Milton's Debt to Greek Tragedy in Samson Agonistes*, The Johns Hopkins Press, 1937

Pattison, Mark. *Milton*, The Macmillan Co., 1879

Pommer, H. F. *Milton and Melville*, University of Pittsburgh Press, 1950

Pope, E. M. *Paradise Regained*, The Johns Hopkins Press, 1947

Rajan, B. *Paradise Lost and the Seventeenth Century Reader*, Chatto & Windus, 1947

Raleigh, Sir W. *Milton*, George Putnam's Sons, 1900

Raymond, D. *Oliver's Secretary*, Minton, Balch & Co., 1932

Sampson, Alden. *Studies in Milton*, Moffat, Yard & Co., 1913

Samuel, I. *Plato and Milton*, Cornell University Press, 1947

Saurat, D. *Milton, Man and Thinker*, The Dial Press, 1925

Schultz, H. *Milton and Forbidden Knowledge*, Modern Language Association, 1955

Sensabaugh, G. F. *The Grand Whig, Milton*, Stanford University Press, 1952

Smith, L. P. *Milton and His Modern Critics*, Little, Brown & Co., 1941

Spaeth, S. *Milton's Knowledge of Music*, Princeton University Press, 1913

Sprott, S. E. *Milton's Art of Prosody*, Blackwell, 1953

Stein, A. S. *Answerable Style*, University of Minnesota Press, 1953

Stevens, H. D. *Milton Papers*, University of Chicago Press, 1927

Stoll, E. E. *Poets and Playwrights*, University of Minnesota Press, 1956

Svendsen, K. *Milton and Science*, Harvard University Press, 1956

Taylor, G. C. *Milton's Use of Du Bartas*, Harvard University Press, 1934

Thaler, A. *Shakespeare's Silences*, Harvard University Press, 1929

Thorpe, J. E. *Milton Criticism*, Rinehart, 1950

Tillyard, E. M. W. *Milton*, The Dial Press, 1930; *The Miltonic Setting Past and Present*, Cambridge University Press, 1938; *Studies in Milton*, Chatto & Windus, 1951

Trent, W. P. *John Milton*, The Macmillan Co., 1899

Van Sinderen, A. *Blake, the Mystic Genius*, Syracuse University Press, 1949

Waldock, A. J. A. *Paradise Lost and Its Critics*, Cambridge University Press, 1947

Warner, R. *John Milton*, Chanticleer Press, 1950

Warren, W. F. *The Universe as Pictured in Milton's "Paradise Lost,"* The Abingdon Press, 1915

Watkins, W. B. C. *The Anatomy of Milton's Verse,* Louisiana State University, 1955

Werblowsky, R. J. Z. *Lucifer and Prometheus,* Routledge & K. Paul, 1952

West, R. H. *Milton and His Angels,* University of Georgia Press, 1955

Whaler, J. *Counterpoint and Symbol,* Rosenkilde & Bagger, 1956

Whiting, G. W. *Milton's Literary Milieu,* University of North Carolina Press, 1939

Williams, C. *The English Poetic Mind,* The Clarendon Press, 1932

Wolfe, D. *Milton in the Puritan Revolution,* T. Nelson & Sons, 1941

Woodberry, G. E. *Great Writers,* The McClure Co., 1907

Woodhall, M. *The Epic of Paradise Lost,* Geo. Putnam's Sons, 1907

Woodhouse, A. S. P. *Milton the Poet,* J. M. Dent, 1955

Editions of Milton's Works

Darbishire, H. *Poetical Works,* The Clarendon Press, 1952-55

Fletcher, H. F. *Complete Poetical Works,* University of Illinois Press, 1943-48

Grierson, H. J. C. *Poems,* Chatto & Windus, 1925

Hanford, J. H. *Poems,* Ronald Press, 1953

Moody, M. V. Houghton, Mifflin Co., 1941

Patterson, F. A. *Ed. Works of John Milton,* 18 Vols. in 21 books. Columbia University Press, 1931-38

Wallace, M. W. *Milton's Prose,* Oxford University Press, 1925

Wolfe, D. M. (Gen. Ed.) *Complete Prose Works of John Milton,* Yale University Press, 1953

Barron's
Simplified Approach Series

The Simplified Approach Series is the key to real understanding and enjoyment of the greatest works of literature.

In a clear, easy style, the editor discusses the great writer as a person to know; tells why and how he was inspired to write as he did; explains customs and historical background to the work itself.

Then he gives a detailed, analytical summary of the work—spiced with direct quotes and allusions—to illustrate the actual style, content and meaning of the work being studied.

95¢ Each

A lively source of material for
discussion · book reports · term papers

ANDERSON:
—Winesburg, Ohio
AUSTEN:
—Pride and Prejudice
BRONTE:
—Wuthering Heights
BUTLER:
—Way of All Flesh
CHAUCER:
—The Canterbury Tales
CONRAD:
—Lord Jim
DANTE:
—The Divine Comedy
DICKENS:
—Bleak House
—David Copperfield
—A Tale of Two Cities
—DOSTOEVSKY
DREISER:
—An American Tragedy
ELIOT:
—Silas Marner
—FAULKNER
—FIELDING
FITZGERALD:
—The Great Gatsby

GOETHE:
—Faust
HARDY:
—The Return of the Native
HAWTHORNE:
—The Scarlet Letter
—HEMINGWAY
HOMER:
—The Iliad and The Odyssey
HUGO:
—Les Miserables
—JAMES
—MANN
MAUGHAM:
—Of Human Bondage
MELVILLE:
—Moby Dick
—MILTON
—MOLIERE
—O'NEILL
—PLATO AND ARISTOTLE
—POE
—ROUSSEAU

SHAKESPEARE:
—As You Like It
—Hamlet
—Henry IV, Part 1
—Julius Caesar
—King Lear
—Macbeth
—The Merchant of Venice
—Othello
—Richard II
—Romeo and Juliet
—The Tempest
STEINBECK:
—The Grapes of Wrath

—Ten Greek Tragedies
THACKERAY:
—Vanity Fair
THOREAU:
—Walden
TOLSTOY:
—War and Peace
—TWAIN
—VERGIL
—VOLTAIRE
—WHITMAN

BARRON'S EDUCATIONAL SERIES, INC.
113 Crossways Park Drive, Woodbury, New York 11797